THE LIFE
IS TOO
SHORT *GUY*

THE LIFE IS TOO SHORT *GUY*

STRATEGIES TO MAKE EVERY DAY THE BEST DAY EVER

SCOTT WHITE

NEW DEGREE PRESS

THE LIFE IS TOO SHORT GUY
Strategies to Make Every Day the Best Day Ever

ISBN   979-8-88504-457-8   *Paperback*
        979-8-88504-481-3   *Ebook*

This book is dedicated to my family. Thank you for being an important part of my Life Is Too Short Guy journey!

To my wife Jenn, my daughters Amanda and Jessica, my parents Joe and Gloria, and Doris and Steve for helping me learn to live every day as the best day ever!

CONTENTS

INTRODUCTION:

THE LIFE IS TOO SHORT GUY

Life is too short, so live your life to the fullest...every second of your life just treasure it...

—WILLIAM SHAKESPEARE

When I was a ten-year-old boy, my dad was my mentor, coach, and role model. He was my friend and my world. He loved to tinker and build things and was very handy around the house. He decided to renovate my brother's bedroom, which seemed like a fun project, and I was his assistant. I couldn't add much value as a child, but together we hung a drop ceiling, put up new paneling, and installed new light fixtures and outlets. And when I say "together," I mean he did the work, and my job was to hold the tools and feel like I was contributing.

We were almost done hanging the last piece of paneling when Dad let out a horrifying scream. I looked up and Dad was tightly grabbing the fingers of his left hand. Dad had sliced his finger while cutting the paneling. It was one of those "sort of bad" cuts. He didn't sever the finger, but it required more than a Band-Aid.

My grandparents lived only a few blocks away. My grandfather, Poppy, was the all-knowing patriarch of the family. While he knew nothing about medicine, his "expert opinion" was that Dad should go to the emergency room and have the cut examined by a doctor. They left together early that evening, and I fell asleep. A few hours later, Mom jarred me awake. As I opened my eyes from a deep sleep, I saw her leaning over me. She tried to catch her breath and said, "Dad had a heart attack while waiting in the emergency room." It turned out it had nothing to do with the injury to his finger; he was in the right place at the right time. He was only forty-two years old and way too young to have a heart attack.

He spent the next week in the hospital. His doctor determined that a number of arteries around his heart were clogged and recommended cardiac bypass surgery. In 1984, not many physicians performed this type of complex surgery, so he and Mom flew to Houston to have one of the leading experts and pioneers in bypass surgery perform the procedure. They were gone about a week. My brother and I stayed with our grandparents and went about our lives as normally as we could. At ten years old, I was unable to comprehend the magnitude of the situation.

I was scared and confused. I hadn't truly appreciated the risk or the complexity of the surgery at that time. About two or three days after the surgery, Mom called and put Dad on the phone. I heard him whisper "Scott," and I cried like never before and probably never have since. I fell to the ground speechless. The floodgate of tears opened, and the cocktail of brewing emotions erupted—a full explosion. This was the moment I realized life is precious and finite. We don't live forever. This was my first major AHA! moment, and it changed my life forever.

The seeds were planted for *The Life Is Too Short Guy*.

WHY SO NEGATIVE?

As I look around the world today, I am disappointed to see negativity everywhere, and I am on a mission to change that. This is my mission because we have so many opportunities to live a happier life.

Why is negativity so prevalent in our society? As a starting point, it is evolutionary. I believe survival in the earliest days of humanity led to a general negativity bias. Our ancestors with the greatest level of fear, skepticism, and pessimism were more astute to daily threats from predators. They constantly had to be aware and alert of predators and risks. This persistent fear and focus on the worst-case scenario kept our early ancestors from being attacked by a bear or a tiger and helped them survive extreme weather conditions. As a result, the gene pools of the most negative survived and were passed on from generation to generation. Those who trusted and didn't fear likely succumbed to the harsh realities of early life.

Survival of the fittest required a certain level of perpetual negativity. As a result, we now live in a world dominated by that same general negativity.

BUT IT SEEMS *SO* BAD

And the reality is, so much of this negativity is logical at a superficial level. We live in a complex world with complicated problems. It's the beginning of 2023, and we just spent almost three years in a world turned completely upside down by the global COVID pandemic. According to the World Health Organization, as of June 2022, approximately half a billion people contracted COVID and over six million died. We had barely emerged from this life-altering COVID experience when the world faced its first significant military action in Europe in decades as Russia invaded Ukraine. Homelessness, food insecurity, poverty, addiction, environmental destruction—the list of global concerns grows every day.

As I rattle off this depressing list of events, it is no wonder people around the world have so much negativity and stress. In a survey conducted by the American Psychological Association and the Harris Poll in February 2022, 87 percent of adults cited inflation as a significant source of stress and 80 percent cited the invasion of Ukraine as a significant source of stress. About three-quarters of survey participants said they were overwhelmed by the number of crises in the world today.

As I dug further, the story got even gloomier. According to an article published by the National Science

Foundation, 80 percent of all thoughts are negative. Not surprisingly, almost 90 percent of media news in the United States is negative (Sacerdote, Sehgal, and Cook 2020). Depression rates have tripled in the two years leading up to 2022, and today suicide is among the top ten causes of death in America (Ettman et al. 2021). According to the National Institute of Mental Health, the rate of suicide has skyrocketed, increasing 35 percent over the last two decades (National Institute of Mental Health 2022).

Whether at home or in the workplace, people just aren't happy. According to a recent study conducted by Monster.com and published in *Insider*, 95 percent of workers said they were considering leaving their jobs and 61 percent of those same workers said they were burned out (Cooban 2021). Most compelling is that during 2020, according to the National Opinion Research Center at the University of Chicago, Americans were more unhappy than they'd been in nearly fifty years. More unhappy than in half a century!

Wow, life sucks! What a miserable world we live in! It's human nature and easier to be negative and to focus on the worst the world has to offer. It is evolutionary. As we reflect on life in 2023, most people believe the world we live in and life in general have never been worse. Most people live with a negativity bias. Most people don't strive to make every day the best day ever. Most people don't proactively cherish their finite time on earth. Most people are wrong.

BUT WAIT, THERE IS DEMAND
FOR HAPPINESS

But you aren't most people. You proactively made the decision to explore a path to greater happiness by reading this book. Even in a world focused on negativity, we all yearn for greater happiness and fulfillment. This is one of the primary reasons I wrote this book. We all want happiness; we just don't make it a priority or even know how to focus on living a happy life. Given how much negativity we currently face, we have massive pent-up demand for happiness. However, too many people do not prioritize happiness. Most of us generally believe, "I will get to it when I get to it." Or we focus on our physical health and neglect our mental health. Happiness is something we yearn for but don't do anything about.

Thus, *The Life Is Too Short Guy: Strategies to Make Every Day the Best Day Ever* was born. I will walk you through my life philosophy, which I call "LITSG," an acronym for "Life Is Too Short Guy." LITSG makes happiness the top priority every day, starting with today. In a world emerging from the COVID pandemic, it seems more people are looking for meaning, purpose, and happiness. Arthur Brooks teaches a class for Harvard MBAs called Leadership and Happiness. The three primary objectives of the class are:

1. Students will create a map of their own happiness, desires, motivations, strengths, and weaknesses. In short, they will know themselves more deeply.

2. Students will learn tactics and strategies to raise their levels of well-being and life satisfaction.

3. Students will learn how to lead others in a way that increases happiness.

According to an article in the *Wall Street Journal* (Ellis 2022), the 180 spots in the class fill up quickly and many students who don't get in attend the lectures virtually or receive recaps from students in the class. The course started in 2020 with seventy-two students and has more than doubled in two years. Here are some of the best and brightest young minds in the world prioritizing the search for happiness. They have proactively and aggressively chosen to use some of their very precious minutes at Harvard to learn how to be happy. Stop looking, and make it happen. Make it a priority. I use every precious minute to make myself and those around me happy. Join me on this journey as we further explore the core principles of LITSG.

Life has never been better. Pause...take a big deep breath, smile, and realize life is too short to spend time focused on the negative. While the vast majority of people look around and see negativity all around them, each person has the ability to find positivity everywhere. I mean everyone and everywhere. You have the ability to find positivity and live a better, happier, and more fulfilling life today.

DON'T WAIT FOR THAT EPIPHANY

For many people, it takes a life epiphany—or more—to escape the doldrums and negativity bias of daily life. People generally go about life without a deliberate focus on happiness, positivity, and gratefulness. And then something happens to change their perspective. I call these AHA! moments. They are the significant, sometimes catastrophic moments when your perspective changes and you make the decision to replace the negativity bias in your life with a positivity bias. While everyone else is wasting precious minutes waiting for life's kick-in-the-teeth, embrace today as your AHA! moment. As you learn about the LITSG philosophy, I hope reading this book will be your AHA! moment.

I am living an amazing life, making the most of every minute. I am the happiest guy in the world. I will have faced, and will continue to face, twists and turns along my journey. Everything isn't always perfect or easy, but with each AHA! moment, my LITSG philosophy evolved. LITSG drives how I think and how I live.

In addition to my dad's heart attack, I had a major AHA! moment while witnessing a commercial airplane crash into the World Trade Center on 9/11, and other AHA! moments when I buried both my mom and dad way too young. I have been blessed to learn from each of these AHA! moments and live a wonderful, happy, and fulfilling life today.

We all have AHA! moments in life, and these moments transform us. As we explore this LITSG philosophy, I will share truly amazing, thought-provoking, life-changing, and extraordinary AHA! moments of ordinary people I interviewed for this book. Many have dealt with major transformative events including illness, addiction, death, and serious injury. All have altered their philosophy on life for the better. You have the opportunity to take these stories and make deliberate choices to change your life philosophy and attitude today. I mean *today* and I am so excited for you.

I want to share this LITSG philosophy with the world. Everyone has the ability to embrace the messages in this book and the principles of LITSG to live a happier life. Whether you are graduating from high school or college, starting your career, plodding along in life without direction or purpose, or recovering from a major life setback, everyone can benefit from LITSG. I mean everyone!

As I reflect on my role in the world and what motivates me, I realize my purpose is to inspire, motivate, and make people happier. I am on a mission to make the world happier, one smile at a time. Simple but powerful. LITSG is my lens for life. I live every day to the fullest. I am grateful for all and find happiness everywhere. It is not merely a belief or an idea. It is not a passing fad. It is not a singular concept. It is a way of living. It is an all-encompassing lifestyle. Like my purpose, it is simple but powerful.

I welcome you to join me on a journey of inspiration, motivation, and transformation of your perspective in a way that can make you happier. Each chapter will focus on a key principle of LITSG and share stories about how I, and others, have seized major AHA! moments to rewrite our life stories. This book is intended to provide practical tools and give you the opportunity to change your life. Each chapter will provide you simple, powerful, and actionable takeaways. You control your own destiny, and you have the ability to live a happier life. Put on a smile. Open your mind. Embrace the principles and enjoy the ride.

Life is too short!

Let's join Life Is Too Short Guy on a journey to make every day the best day ever.

CHAPTER 1:

ROADMAP TO HAPPINESS—MEET LITSG

You grow up and become an adult the day you bury a parent. On March 30, 2007, I lost my close friend, mentor, and confidant—my dad. Two days later, I buried him, and this was one of my greatest AHA! moments. LITSG became abundantly clear to me on April Fools' Day 2007.

As previously mentioned, Dad had a heart attack and triple bypass surgery at forty-two years old. He recovered well and went on to live a full life. However, his heart disease never went away, and unfortunately, he never took it seriously. He "watched" his diet by removing the bacon from his double cheeseburger, and he exercised regularly with a five-minute stroll around the block. He decided he would "beat the system" by trying to starve himself for days before his blood test to "fool" the cholesterol count. Boy, did he fool them. As a result, every seven to ten years, he needed to have stents inserted in his arteries as they continued to clog over time. It was like he was part of the frequent stent club, earning points for prizes he never cashed in!

In late 2006, he could tell something wasn't quite right. He was tired and winded frequently. His cardiologist found a number of clogged arteries and suggested he see a cardiac surgeon. The surgeon recommended bypass surgery again. After much debate with his cardiologist (who opposed the surgery) and the surgeon (who couldn't wait to sharpen his scalpel and cut), he returned to the operating room for another round of bypass surgery.

On a very early and cold March morning, I arrived at my parents' house at 5:30 a.m. My brother Rob was there. We left the house to go to the hospital in two cars, Mom with Rob and Dad with me. Little did any of us realize this would be Dad's last trip in a car—a LITSG moment I only realized upon later reflection. Embrace each minute and each experience; you never know when it will be the last.

We arrived at the hospital and waited while Dad registered. Then they took him away for surgery prep. Before surgery, we went in to see him, gave him a hug, and wished him luck. Mom placed a note in his pocket that said, "Take good care of him. He is one of a kind. There are no copies."

After what felt like an eternity, the doctor came out and said the surgery went well, but he was surprised by how damaged Dad's lungs were. He noted this was probably from the first bypass surgery decades earlier.

When we finally got in to see him in the open-heart recovery area, he was under a heavy blanket with a blue plastic tube attached. He had a breathing tube coming out of his mouth, and his face was very pale. IV bags hung behind him with numerous lines attached to his body. The constant beeping of the various monitors let us know he was alive but clearly in a very vulnerable state. We expected him to be there for a day or two before heading to a recovery room; however, he never made it to recovery.

We all returned the next day, and he was awake. The surgeon explained Dad had a problem with his lungs, and he may have to operate again. Dad wrote a note saying he was "scared." It was the first time I could remember him saying he was scared. This was eye-opening for me and raised my level of anxiety.

The next few days, we took turns visiting him. He knew things were not going well, but he tried to stay positive. He remained in the same bed he was in when he came out of surgery. We talked about random things to keep the mood upbeat and casual. One of the last things I talked about with him was a condo I planned to purchase in an Asbury Park building called The Esperanza. I had received the contract and brought the plans to show him. He pointed to one of the bedrooms and said it was going to be his when he visited. I smiled and agreed. This was Saturday, March 24, the last time I spoke to him. On the TV over his bed, we were watching the Rutgers-versus-Duke women's basketball game in the NCAA tournament. This will forever stay with me as the final memory of my dad awake and interacting.

The next day I returned to the hospital and brought pictures of The Esperanza. Because he had difficulty breathing during the night, he was medically sedated and paralyzed. He never regained consciousness. The nurses told me he could hear me and feel my touch. I held his hand and told him I had pictures of The Esperanza. I told him about the exciting Rutgers win over Duke. I hope he heard me.

Over the next few days doctors tried different types of ventilators, but nothing worked. He remained unconscious in his bed. I touched his arm and reminded him how much I loved him. I told him to stay strong. I hope he heard me then too. By Wednesday his kidneys were failing, and they put him on dialysis.

On Friday, they moved him to a private room in intensive care. I was terrified. The man whose energy infected those around him was now so still, pale, and hollow. Each beep and tick of those machines felt like a countdown to the end.

Around 5 p.m. I told Rob to take Mom home. She was clearly worn down. I called my wife Jenn and told her I would be home for dinner shortly. I hung out for a few minutes on my own and spoke to Dad. It was a quiet moment of reflection, even with all the noise around us. I told him how much I loved him. I left not knowing this would be the last time I would see him alive, but even if I did, I wouldn't have said anything differently. I am grateful all three of us saw him that afternoon.

A little after 10 p.m. I was in bed reading when the phone rang. It was Rob, crying. He said, "Dad is gone." Those words are indelibly marked in my memory. He continued, "The doctor just called. They worked on him for a half-hour. I haven't told Mom yet. They are leaving him in his hospital bed for us to see him." I hung up and fell to my knees as Jenn came over to hug me. In that moment, my world turned upside down.

I walked in circles for a few minutes lost, confused, and without a plan or direction. Jenn wanted to come with me to the hospital. My gut reaction was to decline, but I realized I needed her. We carried two sleeping young children down to the car. We dropped them off at my in-laws and waited for Rob and his wife, Margaret, to arrive with Mom. She got out of the car and was hysterically crying. Behind her walker, she pushed herself slowly up the driveway toward me. Nothing in life could have prepared me for this moment. Here was my mom, frail and devastated, moments after learning she had just lost her best friend and life partner.

We went back to the same room I had just left a few hours earlier. The lights were off, the machines were gone. He was peaceful for the first time in ten days. He lay there motionless, lifeless, cold. Never could I have imagined what my father would look like dead. Now I knew. There he was. Gone forever.

We stayed in the room for a few minutes and cried together. I kept telling everyone he was much better off now, with no more suffering. I hugged everyone hard and told them we were going to make it. Inside, however, I was dying. This was one of the worst moments of my life—an AHA! moment when I realized this was the beginning of a new chapter in my life. We all touched his now-cold body and kissed him goodbye.

The next morning I woke up early and drafted the eulogy. The words poured from my heart as tears dripped on the keyboard. Dad was a truly amazing human being, and telling the world about how great he was turned out to be easier than I expected.

The next task was selecting clothes for him to be buried in. I met Rob and Mom at the house where I grew up. I stood in my parents' bedroom and pulled out shirts, pants, jackets, and shoes from his closet for Mom to consider. What shirt held meaning for him? What jacket did she like? Do we need to bring shoes? Meaningless questions. The tears just kept on flowing.

Then began the process of contacting everyone to share the news and funeral details. Painful calls you never imagine making or ever want to make again.

Sunday, April 1, 2007—the day I buried my father. I did see some irony in it being April Fools' Day. As hard and as sad as it was, I just smiled and tried to laugh. Even on this day, we found humor. We arrived at the funeral home that dreary Sunday. Shortly after us, our friends began to pour in. I was amazed and honored by how many people showed up. It was a real tribute to him and our family.

We saw him one final time. Words cannot convey what it was like to see my father in a casket. For the first time in weeks, he was clean shaven and peaceful. He wore a suit and had his tallit (a traditional Jewish prayer shawl) draped over his shoulders. He had on the yarmulke (a Jewish head covering) from my wedding. Rob pinned a sign language "I love you" pin to his lapel. He had a Boy Scouts hat and a Rutgers hat next to either side of his head. We held hands and tried to comfort each other as we cried.

I delivered the eulogy. Rob stood by my side while Mom sat in the front row. She was heartbroken but proud to see her sons saying kind things about her life partner. Some of his close friends also spoke. Their eloquent words and stories made me cry yet again.

The pall bearers wheeled his body ahead of the procession of mourners. As our car followed the hearse, I made jokes about how he was probably "rolling over" in his casket annoyed we were all making such a big deal. I imagined him saying, "I'm dead. Move on. Don't you have better things to do?"

At the cemetery they unloaded the casket and lowered my dad into the ground. This was the moment of truth, my acknowledgment that he was really gone. The rabbi said a few words and then shoveled dirt on the casket. I was the first to follow with three shovels full. No task can be worse than shoveling dirt on your father's casket. Many of the attendees followed, but Mom could not. She sat on her walker and just cried. She reached down and picked up a handful of dirt and put it in her pocket.

We returned to our house to begin Shiva, the traditional Jewish mourning period. So many people showed up to pay their respects. It helped a little at a very difficult time. This was another LITSG moment as I really understood the power of community and how no one can make it alone. We need each other in good times and especially in challenging times.

A week or two later I started the process of cleaning out my parents' house. Of all the pain associated with the death and burial of my father, cleaning out and emptying the house I grew up in was among the most painful. I slowly sorted through pictures, cards, gifts, and other mementos of my parents' life together. All of these things evoked strong memories for me. For months I spent a few hours each night after work and most weekends going room by room, discarding memories and crying. Friends joined me on weekends, and I can still remember each one who offered support. For me this was the ultimate example of the power of community.

My dad's death, and the subsequent life adjustment, was the biggest AHA! moment of my life. It started with his surgery and continued through his rapid decline, death, burial, and caring for my mom afterward. These events crystallized much of my prior thinking around LITSG. I began to embrace each moment and focused on happiness, positivity, gratitude, and living in the moment. Death had come so close to me, and I truly realized life is too short... Make every day the best day ever!

NOT A CONCEPT OR IDEA... IT REALLY IS A WAY OF LIFE

Forty-two million minutes! Based on an average life expectancy of about eighty years old, we each only have about forty-two million minutes to play with in our lives. And while that might seem like a pretty significant number, as I break it down further, you will realize life is just too short to waste time. Let's have a little fun and do some simple math together.

Let's just assume that over a lifetime we each get about eight hours of sleep per night. I realize this will change at various points in our lives with some people sleeping significantly more as babies, and significantly less in the years when we have a baby. Some will scoff at the thought of eight hours of sleep. As you read this, you might have said, "In your dreams!" But in general, this is a reasonable estimate over a lifetime. So, if you assume about eight hours per day for eighty years, this results in one-third of your life spent sleeping. That means you have to subtract about fourteen million minutes for sleeping and you are down to twenty-eight million productive minutes. Now, I am guessing you are probably not a newborn reading this. If you are, I am really impressed, but let's be realistic. Rather than starting at the beginning, you are somewhere along the spectrum of twenty-eight million minutes.

I am going to take the middle for now. If you are older or younger, you can do some minor adjustments. All of a sudden, you have about fourteen million minutes to choose what to do with. Invariably, most of us will face some level of physical and mental decline as we age. For LITSG math purposes, let's assume the final three years of life are impaired in some way, either physically, mentally, or both. You lose about 1.6 million minutes right there. Wow, now you are down to 12.4 million minutes. And unfortunately, you will spend some time ill each year when you won't necessarily have the ability to maximize the value of those minutes. Hard to make a reasonable guess here, but let's just round out another half a million minutes, and we have about twelve million minutes left. Each person can do their personal math and adjust accordingly, but twelve million minutes, plus or minus, just isn't that long. Twelve million minutes!

I do this math as a wake-up call. It is not a countdown to the end, but rather a call to action. Stop and think about how you measure and use those minutes. Are you making the most of every one of those minutes? Really? Do you want to use them differently going forward?

LITSG makes the most of every minute and lives by this mantra. So at this point, you should be asking, "Who exactly is this crazy Life Is Too Short Guy, and who lives by the LITSG philosophy?" Me! I am the Life Is Too Short Guy, and this is my philosophy on life. However, the beauty of it is that anyone can live by the principles of LITSG. The philosophy is equally applicable to all. It can be used by a middle-aged, reasonably well-educated male or female living in New Jersey or a child embarking on kindergarten and starting an educational journey in Indiana. How about a retired widower in Florida enjoying beautiful weather and the next phase of life? Yup. Or a recent high school graduate, ready to embrace the world? Absolutely. College students? Without a doubt! The list goes on and on. As you read this, realize LITSG is you. LITSG is all of us.

It is important to recognize that not everyone has the same opportunities and good fortune. As you read this you may be thinking that some people (maybe you) have been dealt a really bad hand in life, either at birth or later on. LITSG provides a bridge to greater happiness for all. Regardless of where you start or where you are in life, the principles are still applicable.

Everyone can become LITSG and live a happier, more fulfilled life by embracing the philosophy. LITSG represents a way of life, a way of thinking. It is a way of making every day the best day ever. It is simple but powerful. Let's learn more together.

As you follow me on a journey through this book, two underlying themes help drive me and this philosophy. First, I am full of *energy*. No matter the time or location, I radiate excitement and enthusiasm. Sure, I get tired and need to recover occasionally. Sleep and rest are important. But rather than focus on feeling tired or drained, I focus on the possibility of the moment. I draw on my inner energy to become a prism of energy for all those around me. We each have the ability to find, share, and create energy. Think Energizer Bunny! It is not a physical attribute, but a mental perspective. If you feel tired or worn out, turn the narrative on its head and focus instead on finding someone, something, or some way to energize your attitude.

Second, I am *confident*. Even when I am outside my comfort zone or learning new things, I draw on past success to inspire confidence. Not every situation is comfortable, but every situation is an opportunity to reflect on past success and use those memories as foundations for future success. Be confident. We all have moments of self-doubt, but don't focus on that. I can! I will! I did! I am confident! You must be too. Like energy, confidence comes from within. It is a mental characteristic defined by perspective and attitude.

As I embarked on this writing journey, the aspiring author in me might have said things like, "I have never written a book and have no idea how to," or, "I just don't really know enough about any particular topic to write a book." These thoughts crossed my mind briefly. Very briefly. Rather than allowing them to control the narrative and stop me, I focused on related success and created an internal image and persona of a confident, proven author. I started by focusing on a topic that excited and motivated me and reflected on how I have succeeded in the past. I thought about articles I had written for publication without knowing if anyone would read them. I surrounded myself with tools, coaches, mentors, and other aspiring writers to create an ecosystem of success. I carefully thought about past challenges and identified both successes and failures. Success breeds confidence. Failures create opportunities to learn and do things better the next time.

LITSG is a broad and holistic way of life with ten core principles. As we explore the core principles, one of the key themes I will continue to focus on is that we each only have a finite number of minutes and must allocate these minutes to meaningful and important things. "Meaningful and important" are concepts each person must define for themselves. There is no judgment about how we each define what is meaningful and important. However, at the core of the LITSG philosophy is "life is too short!" So, by definition, LITSG doesn't want to use minutes inefficiently to waste time and energy on things we don't believe are meaningful and important.

Two statements I find myself saying almost every day are "let this be the biggest problem I ever have" and "there are bigger problems in the world." We undoubtedly each face problems, disappointments, and setbacks. It would be intellectually dishonest to pretend everything is perfect. But rather than dwell on the negative or allocate a lot of energy to setbacks and disappointments, LITSG empowers us to put them in perspective relative to "bigger" problems. This does require making judgments and comparisons, but regardless of the situation, a bigger problem *always* exists. Part of the LITSG challenge is to use your attitude to define the magnitude of the problem. By definition, it can always be bigger. So long as you approach each challenge this way, you begin to put your "problems" into perspective and realize wasting your limited time dwelling on them serves you no good.

One of the fun things I do is observe LITSG principles in how others approach life and smile when I see the principles "living and breathing in the wild." As I was writing this book, I hopped into an Uber in Dallas for a short ride to the airport. Little did I know my Uber driver, Michael, would blow my mind with his AHA! moments and further help me appreciate the power of LITSG.

WOW... AN UBER SURPRISE

"How long have you been living in Dallas?" I asked Michael. I like to engage everyone I meet and learn their stories.

"Oh, I don't live here. Just visiting."

It seemed like such a strange response from an Uber driver taking me to the airport. I could just see a cartoon bubble pop up over my head with a bunch of symbols in it. I was perplexed. He had rolled up in a well-worn Mercedes covered in dust. He hopped out to open the trunk and apologized for the dirt. The fact that he was visiting Dallas and driving an Uber was odd. I knew there was more to the story, so I probed.

"How long are you here for?" I asked.

"Not sure," Michael said. He had left his home in San Francisco on his birthday in January and decided it was time to just hit the road. He reached a point in his life where his kids were grown, and he was divorced and not tied to anyone in particular. "It was time for an adventure."

He told his adult kids he would be back in six months to a year, and off he drove. First stop was Los Angeles, where he spent about a month before going on to Phoenix and then Dallas, where I met him in late March 2022. We started talking about my book-writing project, and I told him about LITSG. I asked him about his AHA! moment, and he jumped at the opportunity to tell me about two.

First, he told me about the specific moment that put him on this road to nowhere. He didn't feel a need to stay in San Francisco, or California, for that matter. He put his personal belongings in storage and his journey began. At this AHA! Moment, he realized he wanted to explore a new adventure with no particular roadmap or destination.

"I don't really have a plan. I am visiting friends around the country and seeing where things take me. I can literally drop you at the airport and just keep driving." He said Austin might be next, but with no specific timeline. Austin might be in the cards because of a woman he had recently met in a local pickleball group who was a visiting nurse and moving there shortly.

Michael talked fondly about pickleball and its ability to provide an affinity group and social network in any community. It gave him a foundation, a place of belonging, and a social connection to identify with. This is an example of the power of social networks and community, which I will discuss in a later chapter. He talked about how meaningful it is to have social connections as soon as he rolled into a new town.

Michael's career was far reaching across multiple industries. In his early twenties, he raised money for a presidential candidate. He then went on to a career in international finance before committing to a life as an entrepreneur. His primary area of interest was children's toys, having been a founder, CEO, and chairman of ten different companies.

Earlier in his life, Michael had his first major AHA! moment. I probed further. What had set him on a career as an entrepreneur and now driving an Uber in a city he was just passing through? Why the live-life-by-the-seat-of-his-pants approach? He was energized as he told me about how his true life AHA! moment came in 2002 with the death of his very close friend and former roommate Dan. A Princeton University alum and Rhodes Scholar at Oxford University, Dan went on to a successful career in finance leading a boutique investment bank and then chairing JPMorgan Chase's H&Q division. At forty-three years old, Dan was diagnosed with brain cancer and died fifteen months later.

After his diagnosis, Dan quit work to spend more time with his children from a second marriage. "This was his second group of kids. His first group [of kids], he never saw. But shortly after quitting, he started a foundation that became all-consuming to him.

"After Dan launched the foundation, Michael attended a school play for his sixth-grader son and noticed that even after his diagnosis, Dan wasn't at the performance for his first-grader son. "I said, you know, he just couldn't change stripes. He wasn't there for his son. He didn't have that attitude that life is too short to be there for his son.

I felt so bad for his son. He was a workaholic and didn't know anything else."

In such a short trip to the airport, I learned so much about Michael's fascinating story. It was exciting, motivating, and thought-provoking. I witnessed him living some of the key principles of the LITSG life. As I got out of the car at the airport, Michael wished me a safe journey and yelled out the window as he drove off, "Life is too short!"

THE PERFECT TEN

In gymnastics and diving, the pinnacle of success is scoring a perfect ten. Only the rarest of athletes reach this level of excellence. However, gymnasts and divers aspire to reach this goal.

LITSG is built on a foundation of ten core principles:

1. Attitude is everything: the power of positivity
2. Choose your attitude; own it
3. Little things make a big difference
4. Funny things are everywhere
5. Minutes matter
6. Learn, learn, learn
7. Take a chance and get it done today
8. Can't make it alone
9. Passion
10. Live today; don't wait for tomorrow

As we embark on the LITSG journey together, we will explore each of these ten principles in detail, and I challenge you to strive for a perfect ten. All ten principles might not appeal to you. You may decide only a few of the principles make sense right now. Which principles you choose to pursue may change over time. You will choose how best to go about implementing each of the principles for yourself. These will be different for everyone. But now is the time to take on the challenge and set your goal. Join me on this journey to achieve a perfect ten!

LITSG REFLECTIONS

1. Think about the math around how many minutes you may have left in your life. Write down the number of minutes you likely have left. Are you using those minutes wisely, deliberately, and in a way that makes you happy and feeling fulfilled?

2. Each person has the ability to adopt the LITSG principles to live a happier, more meaningful life. Without knowing much about each yet, which of the ten principles resonate the most with you? Which do you think presents the best opportunities to enhance your happiness and well-being?

3. What is your goal for reading this book? What do you hope to accomplish? Write it down so you can go back to it after reading the book.

4. As you read this book, think about others in your life who can benefit from these principles. Who are they? How can you help them live a happier life?

CHAPTER 2:

ATTITUDE IS EVERYTHING—THE POWER OF POSITIVITY

Keep your thoughts positive because your thoughts become your words. Keep your words positive because your words become your behavior. Keep your behavior positive because your behavior becomes your habits. Keep your habits positive because your habits become your values. Keep your values positive because your values become your destiny.

—MAHATMA GANDHI

We each have the ability to control our own happiness. We *each* have the ability to control our own happiness. We each have the *ability* to control our own happiness. We each have the ability to *control* our own happiness. We each have the ability to control our own *happiness*.

Now that I repeated it, you must realize how important it is. So important it was worth repeating five times. More importantly, note the word I emphasized each time, and think about how it changes the meaning of the sentence. In the end, each word is powerful, and the statement is vital to understanding LITSG.

People debate over exactly how much control we have, but numerous academic studies support the notion that we control our own happiness. In the seminal paper entitled "Pursuing Happiness: The Architecture of Sustainable Change" (Lyubomirsky, Sheldon, and Schkade 2005) published in the *Review of General Psychology*, researchers concluded that about 50 percent of happiness is determined by our genes, 40 percent by our attitude and perspective, and 10 percent by our circumstances. The key conclusion was that we each control about half of our happiness.

In fact, the mere belief that you can control happiness makes you happier. In a 2020 study of 1,144 participants, the survey from Tracking Happiness asked, "Can we control our own happiness?" Eighty-nine percent of respondents believed happiness is something you can control and of those, 32 percent were happier than those who didn't think happiness can be controlled. Respondents with low happiness ratings were five times more likely to feel like they couldn't control happiness compared to people with high happiness ratings.

Okay, enough with the stats. Let's get practical here. The core principle of the LITSG philosophy is that attitude is everything and we each have enormous power to approach the world every day through a lens of positivity. Nothing is more essential to LITSG than this. So, let's explore exactly how to do this.

ONE CHANCE TO START EVERY DAY RIGHT... DON'T BLOW IT

Whether you think you can, or you think you can't—you're right.

—HENRY FORD

Each day is a new beginning. Your first thought each morning is your most important thought. As you approach each day, set out to prove yourself and your first thought right. First impressions matter, and so do first thoughts. As I wake up each day, I proactively smile and practice gratefulness to the extreme. Grateful to be alive. Grateful to wake up next to someone I love. Grateful to have a roof over my head. Grateful to have sight to see the beautiful surroundings. Grateful for the day ahead. Grateful, grateful, grateful. But the choice to make the most of my day and to thrive is my very first thought. This is an important concept of LITSG.

It is not merely about the words but about the specific actions and beliefs tied to those words. I specifically and proactively say things like:

- "Happy Monday (or whatever day it is)."
- "Today is the best day of my life."
- "Happy first day of spring."
- "Happy last day of July."
- "Happy Groundhog Day, Valentine's Day, Thanksgiving, etc."

We always have something to be happy about. Merely saying it out loud proclaims it to the world as a statement of belief. More importantly, *I actually believe it.* Saying it and not believing it is useless. Believing it and not saying it doesn't fully capture the essence and power of the statement. The saying and believing are inextricably linked and the essence of LITSG. Wake up, smile, and say something positive. Simple, but powerful. Try it.

If your first thought is grounded in gratefulness, happiness, and positivity, you have set the right tone for your day. This is your lens to view the world. From this point forward, every minute is a chance for capitalizing on these happy thoughts. Alternatively, if your first thought is one of fear, dread, or negativity, this sadly becomes a cloudy lens for the day. Starting the day with "this sucks" is a big hole to dig yourself out of. As noted in the Henry Ford quote above, if you think something sucks, you are probably right. Why suck? Too often we wake up and our first thought is dread about a meeting, appointment, or dealing with someone that day. Or we may regret what we ate, drank, or did last night. We may fear what will happen today, tomorrow, or even next month. Stop!

You can "clean your lens" and focus on a greater sense of happiness and positivity, but it is so much harder when you have on cloudy glasses to start the day. While there might be curve balls or unexpected twists throughout the day, the clean lens of positivity sets the right tone for the day. Think about reframing negative thoughts or setbacks and instead seeing them in a positive way. Reframe the dreaded meeting as an opportunity to help someone else, coach them, mentor them, teach them. How about gratefulness to be alive, healthy, and gainfully employed? Try focusing on making affirmative statements such as, "I will find happiness, success, and fun in the day ahead."

Every day is a new beginning—a new opportunity to learn, grow, experience, and enjoy life. I don't wait for a new year to have a new beginning. Each season is a new beginning. Each month is a new beginning. Each week is a new beginning. Each day is a new beginning. Of those forty-two million minutes I started with in my life, each minute is a new opportunity to do something special, big, meaningful, and fun.

We started with the foundational premise that attitude is everything and positivity is vitally important to living a LITSG life. We each have the ability to start every day right, find happiness and gratefulness, and view the world through a lens of positivity. Unfortunately, as we will learn throughout this book, too often it takes a major setback or AHA! moment to learn this. This was the case for Steve Guberman.

THE TEENAGER WHO DECIDED TO CHANGE RATHER THAN DIE

"At the ripe old age of nineteen, I literally had to turn my life around. I realized that if I don't make a change, I'll be dead pretty soon."

On January 10, 1996, Steve Guberman's first of two major AHA! moments changed his life and his perspective.

"We grew up in a very middle-class family. And for all intents and purposes, we all were given every opportunity to be successful and do good things, and we were raised to be good people. For some reason, I took a turn in a different direction and ended up barely graduating high school, messed up on drugs, and getting arrested a couple of times, certainly causing chaos and worry and stress in the family."

On his mom's birthday Steve had that AHA! epiphany and decided he had to make a change. He wanted to survive. He realized he was grateful to be alive given the circumstances he had created for himself. "And the fact that I'm not dead, I was like 'Don't look a gift horse in the mouth,'" said Steve. "You need to make something of yourself, do something with your life, help other people, and be a good person."

Steve began his journey of getting clean and sober to earn his way back into his family. He worked hard and committed to making himself better. But deep down, gratefulness drove him more than anything. He realized how lucky he was and changed his life and perspective from one of despair to gratefulness. He owed it to himself, his family, and more broadly, to the world, to give back and help other people.

He committed to the twelve-step recovery program and went to group rehab meetings every single day for the next eight years. He worked hard at multiple jobs including as a forklift operator, a waiter, and a teacher of English as a Second Language (ESL). He found the courage to enroll in community college and slowly built his confidence and self-esteem. For a kid who had struggled to make it through high school, he worked hard through community college and then studied graphic design, graduating with honors from a four-year college.

Shortly after college he met his wife and started his own graphic design agency, which he built into a successful business and later sold. Along the way, he and his wife adopted a son and gave birth to a daughter about fifteen months later. Adversity hit Steve again as he and his wife divorced when the children were about five or six years old.

Steve had overcome so much and created a comfortable life for himself. Then adversity hit again, and this time it was a major "kick in the teeth." The AHA! moment that shaped Steve's life the most happened on February 13, 2020, when his thirteen-year-old daughter Maya died unexpectedly. It was a reflective moment for Steve. "It is something that helps frame really how temporary everything is, and really how short life is and how fragile it is."

Steve acknowledges how hard it has been to recover from the death of his daughter. He accepts his life will never be the same. However, he decided he wouldn't allow it to draw him down a path of perpetual negativity.

"I met parents who—maybe it's their decision or not—but they've allowed it [the death of a child] to cripple their life and they can't move forward. They can only look backward, and they're literally stuck in depression, and sorrow, and heartbreak. And I've made the conscious decision that I can't allow that to be my life. I'm forty-six now, and I've got a long life ahead of me if I choose to have one. And I've got a son to raise."

Steve chose to be proactive and focus on positivity and gratefulness. He realized it could always be worse, and he has found ways to appreciate what he has. As an example, he noted that Maya died just a few weeks before COVID shut the world down. At least 1,500 people showed up at a ceremony to honor Maya. Three weeks later, no one would have been able to be there in person. "I feel an immense amount of gratitude for the timing of things," Steve said.

Steve discovered gratefulness as a recovering addict in 1996, and it became an important part of his perspective on life. However, the death of Maya amplified it.

"You lose something so great as a child and everything sucks. I could think there's nothing to be grateful for. It's really easy to get mired down in that negativity and depression and lack of gratitude. So, you literally have to make that conscious decision every day to get out of bed today. Find ten things to be grateful for. Literally, my arms, my shirt, the dog, the roof. Just find a few things and be grateful for them. Write them down or don't write them down or share them."

Two major life-altering AHA! moments for Steve shaped his perspective on life. He understands life is too short and fragile. As a result, he has proactively and deliberately decided to find happiness and positivity wherever possible. More importantly, he views the world through a gratefulness lens. Fundamental to the core principle of LITSG that "attitude is everything" is that the seeds of gratefulness are planted to grow into the fields of happiness.

GRATEFUL TO BE GRATEFUL

I take gratefulness to an extreme, and it is a key element of the LITSG philosophy. I am so grateful to just have the ability to be grateful. I learned at a young age to appreciate what I have and not focus on what others have. I am certain my dad's heart attack and his untimely death helped crystalize my focus on gratefulness. Everything presents an opportunity to be grateful. Some suggest a "gratefulness journal" to write down three things you are grateful for daily. Maybe in the morning. Maybe at night. A gratefulness journal is a good start but not enough. It sets a low bar and an expectation that you have to work to find gratefulness. You have to allocate time to think about it and work at it. It implies you only have a few things to be grateful for.

The LITSG philosophy sees gratefulness everywhere, all the time. Each day, I am grateful from the second I wake up. I especially am grateful to wake up next to someone I love. In fact, of all the things I am grateful for, my wife, Jenn, is at the top of the list. Along with my daughters Amanda and Jessica, there is nothing I am more grateful for.

Grateful for the opportunity the day presents. Grateful to see and hear and smell and taste. Grateful to be alive.

And the day is only one minute old. Talk about making the most of that minute. Every moment, thought, interaction, and activity throughout the day ahead is an opportunity to be grateful. Nothing is too small to overlook, and focusing on the small things matters. This is why I find a gratefulness journal with a handful of notes to be insufficient. It may be a good start, but I challenge you to think bigger and more broadly to capture the essence of gratefulness everywhere and always.

As the day progresses, I look around and appreciate my good fortune no matter what is happening. Sure, I have setbacks, but it could be worse. Thus, extreme gratefulness. I say, "Thank you, thank you, thank you," constantly. I proactively send notes, emails, texts, and make phone calls to those who have a positive impact on me to say thank you. Sometimes it can be years after someone has done something kind or valuable for me, and I will shoot a quick note saying, "I know it has been a few years, but I am still really grateful for the impact you had on me. Thanks for that gift. In fact, here is a picture of me using it right now. Thanks again."

I recently donated to DonorsChoose, a national nonprofit organization focused on raising funds for teachers and classrooms. I made the donation in honor of Jay Soled, a teacher I had in business school over twenty-five years ago. He had such a positive impact on me, and I wanted him to know it. Imagine the feeling of surprise, happiness, and gratefulness when he received a letter about the donation. Think about the impact I had on him as a return favor for the impact he had on me. This is extreme gratefulness.

When I graduated from law school in 2000, my first job was as an investment banking associate at Citigroup. It was a very difficult and competitive job to get at the time. I went through numerous rounds of challenging interviews. I competed against some of the best and brightest students in the country to get the job and was both shocked and grateful when I got the opportunity. And I do mean shocked. Sometimes I wonder how I tricked the system and got the job.

When I showed up on the first day at work, about eighty other associates started with me. We were the class of 2000 investment banking associates. All were at the top of their academic classes. All were from the very best schools in the country. All were incredibly competitive and focused on getting into the "right" groups and the "right" assignments for success. All had been preparing for this job for many years, possibly even since birth. This was their dream job and only the best (and somehow, I) were offered investment banking opportunities.

Many of my classmates looked down on menial tasks in favor of high profile and "important" assignments. I had a very, very different approach. I came from a nontraditional background and truly believed I was so lucky to have the opportunity. I had gone to Rutgers Business School a few years earlier and at the time I was interviewing, I was attending the University of Pennsylvania Law School. The top investment banks were generally not recruiting at law schools then. I was a bit of an anomaly interviewing while in law school. Like I said, I did sometimes think it was a mistake. They didn't really intend to offer me a job, but due to an administrative error, here I was as a newly minted investment banker.

I was so grateful every day I walked into the building (and sometimes I would not leave the building for days), that I smiled and whistled happy tunes whenever I walked through the lobby. I continued whistling and smiling on the elevator and then at my desk. I was willing to do anything. And I mean anything (legal). No task was beneath me. I was happy to make copies, bind books, proof documents, and I even joked that I would clean bathrooms and wash the windows if I had to. Whatever task I was asked to do, I would do with great pride and seek to exceed expectations. I was happy and grateful and couldn't believe I had the opportunity. I never thought I was too good for a task. And some tasks were pretty lousy. Five years later, 90 percent of my starting class was gone. Some left on their own, but most were let go. I remained on as one of the very few bankers to make it five years. Gratefulness and a positive attitude were the keys to my success.

I have had a few major AHA! moments that helped me learn the importance of gratefulness. I must admit, I didn't always fully appreciate it at the time. Sometimes we have life-altering AHA! moments without realizing it until much later in life. My close friend Sean Waller believes he lives a life of extreme gratefulness in part because of illness early in his life. But he didn't realize it until a quarter-century later.

LIFE-AFFIRMING MOMENT AT
THIRTY THOUSAND FEET

It was his first time on a private jet. He was en route to his college roommate Bill's funeral. During a deep conversation with his other college roommate Jeff, Sean was shocked to realize how his own childhood cancer had changed his perspective on life. Sean is an elementary school teacher and author of two books. It took many years, but Sean discovered why he was grateful long after his sickness and recovery.

At the age of twelve, Sean was sitting bored in his eighth-grade class flipping his head from side to side when he realized he couldn't hear well out of his right ear. He told his mother that evening. She was already taking his brother to the doctor the next day. Sean tagged along, and after the doctor looked in his ear, he told his mom they should see an ear, nose, and throat doctor. The ENT looked in his ear and suggested a biopsy. Less than two weeks after sitting in class bored and flipping his head aimlessly from side to side, Sean was having surgery to remove a cancerous tumor from his nasal cavity.

After enduring twenty-five radiation treatments and fifteen months of chemotherapy, Sean was a freshman in high school and done with cancer. But he never realized how it impacted him. Not then and not for a quarter-century.

Twenty-five years later, he was jolted by the death of his college roommate, Bill. "He was probably the greatest guy I have ever known," said Sean.

When 9/11 happened, Bill drove from his home in Virginia Beach to Ground Zero in New York City the day of the attack. He was an army medic who wanted to contribute, and he spent several weeks at Ground Zero helping out. This selfless act later led to the disease that killed him.

On the way home, Sean had his life-changing AHA! moment. "Somehow, we got really philosophical for the first time ever. And I don't remember how it came up."

Jeff said, "You are the most optimistic, positive person I've ever met. I have always attributed that to the fact that you almost died when you were a kid. And now every day is a gift. So, you just appreciate it."

Sean was shocked to hear this. "I said, no. I've never thought about that once in my life. Really! I never thought that, but since that moment, I've never *not* thought about that. I don't know if he's right, but I run with it every day. I do feel that way—every day, every day. I was so shocked that he said that to me. Not in a bad way. I was like that makes so much sense to me in my life."

Sean calls that day on the plane with Jeff "life affirming," and since then, he realizes why he is always so positive. Sean specifically focuses on his obligation to be a role model and to live his best life possible. "I do feel a bit of a responsibility to really live up to that. I was lucky. I survived my illness, and I truly feel that I have to earn it."

Sean now lives a life of positivity. This is one of the most important principles of LITSG. My extreme positivity continues to be a major advantage for me throughout my life.

THE HAPPINESS ADVANTAGE

I have placed great emphasis on the importance of attitude with a focus on positivity. Why? Well, because it is foundational to the LITSG philosophy. This is the most important key pillar that the remaining principles are built upon. If you have any doubts, the science is compelling. While I am focused more on the practical application of LITSG, let me spend a few moments backing it up with some fun stats.

In his book *The Happiness Advantage: Linking Positive Brains to Performance* (2010), Shawn Achor makes a compelling case for the power of positivity and the impact it can have. According to his research, 90 percent of long-term happiness is predicted not by the external world, but by the way your brain processes the world. Further, only 25 percent of job successes is predicted by IQ. Seventy-five percent is predicted by optimism levels, social support, and your ability to see stress as a challenge rather than a threat. A positive brain performs significantly better. Your intelligence rises, your creativity rises, your energy level rises. A positive brain is 31 percent more productive. Wow—pretty compelling, don't you think?

Shawn talks about the power of positivity. "It's not the reality that shapes us, but the lens through which your brain views the world that shapes your reality. If we can change the lens, not only can we change your happiness, but we can also change every single business and educational outcome."

WATCH OUT... IT'S EVERYWHERE! REALLY, EVERYWHERE

Life has highs and lows, no way around it. As much as I find happiness and gratefulness everywhere, life sometimes kicks you in the teeth, or maybe somewhere else. Life events like births and birthdays and graduations have natural highs, and sickness and death have natural lows. Using LITSG, I can find happiness and gratefulness everywhere, regardless of the situation. As I discussed in the introduction, one of the most challenging things I have ever done in my life was delivering the eulogy at my father's funeral. Well, here is how I opened the eulogy:

Thank you all very much for coming. Your presence here today is so meaningful to us. On behalf of my mom Gloria and my brother Rob and our families, I want to take a few moments to remember my dad. Only a few hours after his death I sat down to write this. It is one of the hardest things I have ever done in my life.

As I discussed earlier, Dad had a heart attack and triple bypass surgery twenty-three years ago. Rob and I were just old enough to understand the situation but not necessarily mature enough to comprehend the seriousness of it. Well, Dad pulled through that one and we were thankful regularly for it. I remember actually stopping to think at various special times in my life how lucky I was to have two wonderful parents to be there with me. Whether it was my bar mitzvah, wedding, or births of my daughters, I often stopped and thought, "Thank God Dad made it through that surgery in 1984."

While it is appropriate to mourn today and share in our sorrow, I need everyone to stop and do me a favor. Do your best to be happy and be thankful. That's right. Moments before I bury my beloved father, I am asking you all to put a smile on your face and be happy and thankful. Happy for all the times we had with him. Thankful he lived as long as he did. He could have left us many years ago and missed all of the milestones we shared together. For his being here as long as he was, I am happy and thankful. You may find it odd that I emphasize the importance of being happy and thankful. For those who knew my dad well, you understand why I am asking this. It is quintessentially who he was and what he was about.

Wow—check that out. Could you imagine hearing a more positive introduction to a eulogy? Look at how many times I talked about being happy and thankful. How about a call to action to smile at a funeral? Crazy. This is what LITSG is all about. The key themes of this eulogy were happiness and gratefulness. If I could find happiness and gratefulness there, we all can find it everywhere. Look around today. I challenge you.

LITSG REFLECTIONS

1. We each have the ability to control our own happiness through our attitude and perspective. Through what lens do you predominantly view the world? Is there a better lens?

2. Your first thought of the day is a critical first step to finding greater happiness. What was your first thought today? Will you have a positive first thought tomorrow? Did you start your day with a smile?

3. Make sure you share positive thoughts with others. What positive statements did you make today? What positive statements can you make now or later today?

4. Make gratefulness a foundation to your perspective and how you view the world. How often were you aware of your gratefulness today? As you look around now, what are you grateful for? What can you do tomorrow to be more grateful?

5. Think of a time when you faced a difficult situation recently. How could you reframe the situation from one that is negative to one that is positive?

CHAPTER 3:

CHOOSE YOUR ATTITUDE... OWN IT

Nothing can stop the man with the right mental attitude from achieving his goal; nothing on earth can help the man with the wrong mental attitude.

—WINSTON CHURCHILL

You, and solely you, have complete control of your attitude. You own it. It is unique to you. You can't blame anyone for it. You can try, but in the end, the buck stops with you. Attitude is yours and yours alone and is another core foundational principle to LITSG. As discussed previously, positivity is crucial and powerful for making every day the best day ever. Now let's take the philosophy one step further and dig deeper. Take positivity and mix in a little attitude, and you have a powerful elixir.

Every day, we interact with the world around us in so many different ways. We send emails, post on social media, make phone calls, and talk to friends and strangers. Each interaction gives us a chance to choose our attitude and set the tone for us and those around us. I am thoughtful and proactive in setting a positive tone for each interaction, regardless of the situation. I get more out of life by creating ongoing positive interactions with the world around me.

I coached my daughter Jessica's soccer team when she was about eight years old. At the beginning of *every* practice and game, I would say, "It is a beautiful day to play soccer." Some days were spectacular with beautiful sunshine and moderate temperatures, but others were more challenging. This didn't matter to me, and my mantra was always the same. We played in rain, hail, snow, extreme cold, wind, and every other weather combination. It didn't matter because every soccer day was the same to me. "It is a beautiful day to play soccer." Now, a decade later, I still see kids and parents from that team, and they remember that mantra and laugh as they repeat it to me.

LITSG actively seeks opportunities every day and everywhere to choose a positive attitude and set a positive tone, thus creating an atmosphere to make every day the best day ever. What about contentious situations? Can you set a positive tone in a confrontational interaction?

EVEN WHEN THEY WANT TO FIGHT

I am the chairman and CEO of a public real estate company, and sometimes it feels like every day can lead to a fight. Earlier in my career I spent time on Wall Street in investment banking and asset management. I am trained as a lawyer and an accountant. I have spent an entire career in complex business deals and negotiations. Sadly, I have spent too much time on business and legal disputes. Sometimes it feels like everyone wants to fight. Rather than seeking to create value and stronger relationships, we live in a society that seems to focus more on disagreement. The ultimate winners in this context are usually the lawyers who bill by the hour and don't always look for a path to resolve disputes quickly and easily. This runs counter to the principles of LITSG.

It all starts with attitude and tone. As I think about so many of the disputes I have faced over the years, the starting point is usually an email or written correspondence. Too often, disputing parties want to aggressively attack each other in writing. People tend to be much more aggressive and, quite frankly, more obnoxious in writing than over the phone. And when those same people get in a room, they are generally more cordial than when they were on the phone. It is fascinating to watch how tough people are with a keyboard at their fingertips. Take away the keyboard and they wilt. So, whenever you have the opportunity to resolve a dispute, make the effort to meet in person.

Written communication is a convenient curtain to hide behind and to be more aggressive. However, given practical implications and efficiency, in the real world, so many disputes are often discussed via email. This is the worst path to resolution and often leads to escalation. But it doesn't have to be that way. Start by setting the right attitude and tone in your emails. I was recently involved in a business dispute and could have easily started the dialogue with an email that read something like this:

Dan,

I received your notice of termination earlier this week, and I was both surprised and disappointed. This is just another example of where you seem to take every opportunity to escalate the relationship in a negative direction. As you may recall, you were the one who wanted to set the payment structure up like this. Now you are choosing to terminate the relationship in part because of various disagreements among us. I find this behavior to be disturbing, quite frankly. If you want the investors to get paid, please send me the list of investors and their holdings ASAP.

Regards,
Scott

This would have been a rational email based on the dispute I was dealing with. These thoughts crossed my mind briefly. It would have been a follow-up to an aggressive email I received. But I never sent that email. Actually, I never even considered sending it. I sent this instead:

Good afternoon, Dan. Apologies for the delayed response. We had board meetings Tuesday and yesterday. I just returned to New Jersey, and I am now beginning the massive email dig-out.

I received your notice. While I sincerely appreciate you acting as the point of contact (and wish you would reconsider and continue), I respect your decision. Can you please provide us

*with the underlying investor list so we can begin to set up a
system to make the payments?*

*Also, I see you have a Dallas address now. I guess you moved to
warmer weather. Good for you. Probably a lot nicer there today
than in New Jersey. My daughter is actually going to be an
intern at The Four Seasons there this summer. Is that near you?*

*I would be happy to meet in person. Let me know if you want
to discuss this or anything else.*

Be well.
Regards,
Scott

Stop and re-read both emails. Both could be a rational
response to the same fact pattern. Both convey a similar message but with a vastly different tone. How often
would you have sent the first one? How often have you
received an email like the first one? As you think about
living the LITSG life, before jumping on a keyboard and
banging out an aggressive email, pause, take a deep breath
or two (or maybe more), and consider your attitude and
tone. Think about what type of email you would want to
receive and craft your tone and message that way. Don't
use your keyboard as a weapon. Rather, use it as a tool for
building a relationship focused on positivity.

YOU ARE A LEADER... CHOOSE WISELY

LITSG implores leaders to be proactive in setting a positive tone, in part because of their position.

As a leader, you set the tone for those who follow. You have real responsibility, so take it seriously. Leadership comes in so many forms. Parents are leaders who set the tone for their children. Teachers are leaders who set the tone for their classroom. Managers are leaders who set the tone for their team. Leadership is broadly defined to mean those who have the ability to influence others. We are all leaders at various times.

If you have leadership responsibility, you should choose your attitude and tone carefully. You have the ability to impact those you lead, and they have an ability to impact those they lead, and so on. It is a trickle-down effect with far-reaching and important implications. If a manager sets the wrong tone for an employee, that employee then goes home and sets the wrong tone with their spouse who then sets the wrong tone with their kids. Leaders must be thoughtful, proactive, and deliberate in choosing a positive attitude and setting a positive tone.

As the CEO of my company, I send regular notes to my team. I use these notes to convey positivity and develop culture. In February 2022, I was crafting a note and tried a little social experiment to prove this point.

I sent the following memo to my team:

It's really cold! It's dreary and miserable. It's the middle of winter. The days are very short. The temperatures are low. February 1 may very well be one of the most challenging days of the year. Not much daylight. A long way from the fall season and what seems like a very long way to spring. No really great, fun holidays in January or February. We are homeless. We don't have an office. We haven't seen each other in person in months. We are dealing with a number of meaningful challenges in our portfolio and in our industry. COVID lingers and lingers. Every day seems like a new fire to fight. At times it feels hopeless and draining. This just sucks and I am tired.

Today is the best day of my life! The sun is shining. I work with an amazing team. I am truly inspired by and appreciate each of you. I am grateful for our company and you being a part of it. I am truly grateful to be alive and healthy and smiling. I am fired up and motivated to conquer the opportunities we have ahead of us. I love the intellectual stimulation of working with you to win. We are making considerable progress on many fronts. We made so much progress in 2021 and our plan for 2022 is robust. Our new office is going to be amazing. I anxiously await our arrival there and the "relaunch" of our company. Life couldn't possibly be better.

Go ahead and re-read each again. Both are factually accurate. Both are exactly 125 words. Both use the same font. Same situation, same number of words, vastly different perspectives. I will tell you, I struggled with the first paragraph, and it took me considerably longer to write. It's not easy for me to find the negativity lens. The second one flowed quickly and naturally. I had to keep adding words to the first, and I had to cut down the second a lot because I couldn't come up with enough for the first paragraph. It was a challenge to match the word counts exactly, but I did it.

So, as you read this, which are you? Did you wake up today feeling like the first paragraph or the second paragraph? How do you feel most days? I wake up every day feeling like the person writing the second paragraph. While everything is not perfect, every minute I have an opportunity to have a positive impact on those around me, and that is core to who I am. By extension, I believe this is core to who we are as a company. Go embrace today and choose a positive attitude and tone.

I used this memo to encourage my team to choose their attitude. It was a reminder that we each have to own it and choose how to approach attitude. On my LITSG journey, I met Nick Strand and was inspired by how he used his AHA! moments to tell the world how important it is to choose your attitude.

"CHOOSE YOUR ATTITUDE. CREATE YOUR LIFE!"

Nick's mother survived only three months after her lung cancer diagnosis. He watched his wife Brianna slowly die over a decade of battling cystic fibrosis.

Nick Strand is a production manager and lighting director who met his wife at a Future Farmers of America Conference in 2007. She took the stage in front of 3,500 attendees to deliver an inspirational speech and ended it with, "How do you live a full life, day by day, second by second? What's your motivation? What gets you up in the morning? For me, it's living with cystic fibrosis. I was diagnosed with it at age three, and since that time, the reality of not living as long as others has always shaped my outlook on life." Nick was captivated by her. They fell in love and lived an amazing life together for the next decade before cystic fibrosis took her life in May 2017.

Then two years after her death, he woke up one morning and the left side of his face was completely paralyzed. Scared, he ran to "Dr. Google." After a self-diagnosed stroke was ruled out by a professionally trained doctor, he learned he had Bell's palsy. "It's not a stroke; it's not something bigger. So, that was kind of my AHA! moment. If not now, when? So, I was like, 'Well, my brain could go, my lungs could go, my heart could go, and all of a sudden, this story is not there. I have not shared my story or, better yet, Brianna's story.'"

Nick spent sixteen hours a day for the next five weeks and wrote Brianna's story. At this moment he realized how precious time was, and he didn't want to waste any more of it. He also finally realized what his wife's most enduring legacy would be as he looked down from his keyboard to his forearm. The tattoo read, "Choose Your Attitude. Create Your Life!" Of all the wonderful memories and lessons learned over his decade with Brianna, this was the inspiration to change his life and his attitude forever.

Brianna loved quotes. She would find quotes and write quotes. She would cut them out and cover the entire refrigerator with them. Every morning the refrigerator would have new quotes on it. People even visited just to see the new quotes. After the passing of Nick's mom, Brianna wanted to create a special quote for her. She wrote, "Choose Your Attitude. Create Your Life!" on a piece of paper and wrote Nick's mom's name next to it.

"Every single morning you wake up, and no matter how shitty your life is, or how shitty your life was, or how shitty of a decision you made, you have the choice to choose what you're going to do with your life. So, you can either sit there and mull about and just do nothing, or you can make it into something," Nick Strand emphasized this to me as he shouted into his camera during our Zoom call. This was the turning point in his life. After spending over two years mourning Brianna's death, the quote and its meaning transformed him.

He threw himself into his project of writing a book and creating a brand around Choose Your Attitude. With limited experience and a self-acknowledged weakness around writing, he gave it his all and did not quit until he was done. He wrote a book called *Loving Someone Who Is Dying*, drew an image and designed a logo, built a website, and created merchandise to sell on the website. He rented a hall and planned a major book launch event for April 7, 2020. He had invested most of his life savings into this project. Then, on March 10, 2020, he received an email telling him he would have to delay the book launch because COVID was spreading rapidly and no one knew what to expect.

As a "roadie" in the entertainment business, Nick quickly realized his primary source of income would disappear as the entertainment industry went on hiatus due to COVID. Without future income and all of his savings invested in building the Choose Your Attitude brand, Nick faced another challenge. But this time, he was more prepared than ever before.

He lived in his car for a few days and then moved back home with his dad. "It was a very difficult time, and I had to literally, again, choose my attitude." Nick has faced more than his fair share of hardships and setbacks. Yet with each setback, he has a clearer vision of his life and his attitude. He appreciates each minute of life and finds happiness where others might find sorrow. He takes control and chooses his own attitude.

Nick is still trying to build the Choose Your Attitude brand and sell his book. As I think about the importance of attitude and tone to living a LITSG life, I reflect on the setbacks Nick dealt with in his life. After dealing with the deaths of his mother and wife and then dealing with serious financial constraints as a result of COVID, Nick continues to quote Brianna by reminding me, "Choose your attitude. Create your life!"

Part of choosing your attitude means choosing how you interact with the world around you. This includes friends, relatives, colleagues, and even strangers. We interact daily with so many people we have never met before. This is a LITSG opportunity to choose your attitude and get to know the world around you. I will talk to and listen to anyone. Not sure they all want to talk to me, but I give it my best shot.

EVERYONE HAS A STORY... A HUMAN STORY
When was the last time you got to know a stranger? How often do you see a human with a story when you interact with a salesclerk, waiter, or customer service

representative? Well, today is the day to start. LITSG empowers each of us to set a positive attitude and tone with *everyone*. Start with people you don't know. Instead of just seeing a stranger or service provider, see a person with goals, dreams, and aspirations. We all have a story, and we all want to share that story. We all love talking about ourselves. As we learned during COVID, we all crave human interaction and yearn to share our story with others.

I called a customer service hotline for a major airline recently. When Stephanie answered, she started with, "Thank you for calling; how can I help you?" I am going to guess that at least 99 percent of the callers Stephanie engages with respond with something like, "I need to change my flight…" or "I need to change my seat…" or "I need to book a flight…" In most cases, the conversations lead with "I need." As Stephanie spends an entire day hearing "I need" and returns the next day and the next day for more "I need," how do you think Stephanie feels? Stephanie has a "need" too.

Using LITSG principles, when Stephanie asked me how she could help, I responded with, "Good morning, Stephanie. How are you doing today?" In the first ten seconds of the interaction, I have already changed the tone of the conversation. First of all, Stephanie didn't immediately hear "I need," and that already changed everything. And when I asked her, by name, how she was, it was not a passing throwaway question, but I actually made it clear I wanted to know who she was. She responded with surprise and enthusiasm. Someone had acknowledged her and treated her with respect.

Before getting into why I was calling, I used humor to let her know I was a complicated customer with complicated needs, and I could tell she was the right person to help. I needed sophistication to help with complication. She was already engaged and intrigued to want to help.

I asked her more questions than she could ask me. Long before we got to what I needed, I learned she lived in Chicago and had worked for the airline for over a decade. I learned she was married with three children, all in their twenties. I learned two of her children had graduated college, and the third was in college. I learned she had concerns about how one of her children handled money and how this was similar to concerns she had with her aging father. I learned her mother was deceased. I listened and learned about the careers of her husband and children. I created an opportunity for Stephanie to feel like a human being and share her story. I created a positive situation with a positive tone and shared my positive attitude. Stephanie was thrilled and went out of her way to help me. Twice during the call, she put me on hold to talk to "the pricing desk" to get me better pricing. Why? Because Stephanie felt valued. Stephanie felt like a human being and had a chance to share her story.

The same principles apply to strangers. Strangers are merely friends we have not yet met. When I meet people on planes, waiting in line somewhere, or just out and about in daily life, I try to find ways to engage with them. We all have a yearning for belonging and human interaction. LITSG acknowledges everyone has a story and wants to feel appreciated.

Too often we fail to see strangers and service providers as humans and potential friends. As you own your attitude and control how you use it, be proud to interact with the world around you. With billions of people on earth, we have billions of stories to learn. Proactively learn as many stories as you can. You may be surprised about how interesting newly discovered friends can be.

LET'S HAVE SOME FAMILY FUN

The COVID pandemic abruptly shut the world down in 2020. We stayed in our homes and lost opportunities for social interaction. For some people this became stressful and depressing. For my family, however, this became an opportunity for extra fun. We chose our attitude and owned it. We embraced being together and took it to the next level by creating major dinner events in our home. Each night for weeks we had themed dinners.

We started with geographic or cultural themes like Italian, Mexican, and Asian-inspired meals. But rather than just prepare food related to the theme, we dressed up in costumes, decorated the house, and played music relevant to the theme. Once we worked our way through cultural foods, we moved on to other themes like Disney night, '60s night, college night, and formal night. For Disney night I dressed as Prince Charming, Jenn as the Queen of Hearts, and the girls as other Disney characters. Even our dog Scooby was sporting a costume. Each night we would post pictures of our adventures on social media, and we quickly had a following of friends and family waiting to see what the next night would bring. Not only were we having fun, but we helped others find happiness in difficult times. One person commented on social media, "These posts really brighten my mornings!"

YOU ARE YOUR BEST COACH

Life's battles don't always go to the stronger or faster man. But sooner or later, the man who wins is the man who thinks he can.

—VINCE LOMBARDI

Setting the right positive attitude and tone in the world around you starts with *you*. For the sake of importance, I will repeat it again: Own your attitude. You are your own best coach, and LITSG believes positive self-talk has meaningful power. As discussed, attitude is such a key determinant of success or failure. Self-talk perpetuates that attitude.

I regularly say, "I can do this." I push away negativity and self-doubt from my mind. I have trained for and run fifteen marathons and an Ironman triathlon. In all cases I trained hard and constantly chased my personal best. As my training progressed and got harder, my legs hurt and my psyche became tired. Uninspired humans may have given up or begun to think negative thoughts. Not Life Is Too Short Guy! I proactively avoided asking, "Why are you doing this?" or "Can I really get this done?" but rather continued with four simple words: I can do this. No doubt, no room for questions or uncertainty. As I write this book and share my thoughts on LITSG,

I continue to repeat, "I can write this book and make the world happier one smile at a time. This book and the LITSG philosophy will make the world a better place." I avoid asking myself about my ability to write the book and get it done. I can do this!

Note, I use the first-person "I" and not the third person "you" or "Scott." We benefit psychologically when saying, "I can do this, I can get this done, or I can accomplish this." It is considerably more meaningful than statements like, "C'mon, I know you can do this," or, "Scott can do this." Self-talk has the power of taking a difficult or seemingly insurmountable task and making your brain your "strongest muscle." Self-talk sometimes leads to self-doubt. This too is powerful, but in a harmful way. Questioning your ability or telling yourself you can't do something often becomes a self-fulfilling prophecy.

LITSG emphasizes the importance of having a positive attitude and setting a positive tone with all interactions. This starts with me. I have the ability to set the right attitude and tone, and so do you. Choose your attitude and own it!

LITSG REFLECTIONS

1. Your tone in written and verbal communication is so important. How often do you start or respond to an email or text with an aggressive, negative approach? When was the last time you changed the tone to something considerably more positive?

2. Everyone has an opportunity to lead at some point. What have you done to set a positive tone when leading others? How can you set a more positive tone today?

3. Today is the day to make a new friend. Find a stranger and engage with her. Learn her story. How about a service provider? Next time you call someone for assistance, get to know him as a person first. Learn his story and what makes him who he is. What matters to him and what does he care about?

4. You are your own best coach. Setting the right attitude and tone starts with *you*. Own it. Think about a big challenge you are dealing with. What is your self-talk mantra? What are you telling yourself? Avoid doubt or negative thoughts.

CHAPTER 4:

THE HARVARD MODEL UN SHIRT—LITTLE THINGS MAKE A BIG DIFFERENCE

Sometimes the smallest things take up the most room in our heart.

—WINNIE THE POOH

If it's good enough for Winnie the Pooh, it's certainly sage advice for me and you. Small things matter a lot. Little, easy changes to behavior have meaningful impacts on outcomes and attitudes. LITSG focuses on small things with big outcomes. These small things become natural habits and a way of living. You don't have to make major changes to live a happier life. Start small. Smiling, using positive symbols, whistling and singing, random gifts or acts of kindness, and celebrating often are things we can each do to live a happier and more fulfilling life. Big changes are hard and scary. Small changes are easy and meaningful. Let's get started today.

Jenn called me on June 28, 1990, and said she really wanted to go see a movie but didn't have anyone to go with. She clearly had a plan but came across as playful and aloof. We had developed a friendship in chemistry class over the prior few months, and this was the opportunity to become more than friends. I was excited but had to play it cool too. We had been flirting with each other for months in high school. Just a few weeks before, I saw her at a local restaurant celebrating her birthday. I went over to her and wished her luck on her driver's license test. I felt a spark, but I wasn't sure where to take it.

Wow! With this call, she opened the door, and I bolted right through it. "I would love to go see *Gremlins 2*," I told her. I had absolutely no interest in *Gremlins 2*, but I had interest in anything Jenn wanted to do. So, I hung up and scrambled to my shirt drawer to choose appropriate attire for this cinematic masterpiece. My wardrobe wasn't very extensive or sophisticated, but after careful consideration I selected my Harvard Model United Nations T-shirt.

Earlier in the year I had been selected to join a "prestigious" group of model United Nations "athletes" to spend a few days at Harvard solving the world's most pressing problems. To a sixteen-year-old about to embark on his first date, this T-shirt said it all. Do you know how cool I am? I mean, I was among the elite chosen from our high school class to represent our school at one of the most elite academic institutions in the world. Surely, she will be impressed. I put on that fancy blue Harvard Model UN T-shirt and waited for her to pick me up. I didn't have a license yet. She was older, had a license, and a car. Jackpot. I had my cool Harvard Model UN T-shirt.

Well, that date turned into many more and exactly six years after that first date, we got engaged on June 28, 1996. Every single year on June 28 for the last thirty-plus years, I take that fancy blue Harvard Model UN T-shirt out of the drawer and put it on. If I could impress her on the first date with it, I am sure I can impress her each year for the subsequent decades. Right? What is most impressive is that I still have it and it still fits!

What really matters is the power of the T-shirt. The T-shirt is a symbol of happiness, fun, love, longevity, and togetherness. The T-shirt is a celebration of another year together. "Little things make a big difference" is a key principle of the LITSG philosophy, and this little T-shirt has created many happy moments and memories for both of us.

KINDNESS RANDOMLY

As a Jersey guy, it was time for a party at the Jersey Shore. Jenn and I took our daughter Jessica and her friends to dinner to celebrate her sixteenth birthday. We chose a casual restaurant with an active outdoor courtyard. A band played pop music and patrons played games like darts and cornhole. Jenn and I sat at our own table and consumed a beverage or two with some unhealthy appetizers as I glanced at a young couple enjoying dinner across the restaurant. I guessed they were in their early twenties, on a date for at least the third or fourth time, and were introduced to each other by a common friend who was hoping to be the magical "matchmaker." That may not have been true, but I created my own fun story.

They reminded me of Jenn and me early in our relationship. As they ordered dessert, I called over the waitress. I gave her my credit card and asked her to charge their dinner to us. A few minutes later the lovely couple came over to thank us profusely. The small gesture made us incredibly happy and made this couple even happier.

A great time to surprise people with kindness is when they least expect it.

On a family vacation to Cabo on Christmas Day in 2021, Jenn came up with the idea of giving small gifts to the flight attendants as a gesture to say thank you. Along with my daughters, she assembled a dozen or so small plastic suitcases filled with candy, lip balms, Starbucks gift cards, and assorted gifts. As we boarded the plane, we handed one to each of the flight attendants. Their eyes lit up, and they grinned and thanked us. Flight attendants are in the category of service providers I discussed earlier. They deal with a lot of heartache and unhappy customers and are rarely recognized or treated with compassion. We did the same thing on a subsequent trip, and that flight crew handwrote a thank-you note to us. Very small gesture, very big impact.

While I am a big believer in performing random acts of kindness, I have also been the recipient of them. I could not have been more surprised or grateful than when a stranger helped me get across my first marathon finish line.

"Someday I will do a marathon," I vowed as a teenager. I enjoyed running. I had run some local 5K and 10K races and was on my high school track team. My teenage years turned into my twenties, and then my thirties hit. It was time to make the leap and register. Consistent with one of the LITSG principles, it was time to take a chance and get it done today. After two or three months of running a few miles per week, on February 16, 2005, I applied for entry to the New York City Marathon.

I ramped up my mileage and was running more and training harder, but I didn't tell anyone as I didn't know if I would actually get in. The New York City Marathon, like other major marathons, uses a lottery system for entrance, and every year, it gets harder to get in. February rolled into March, and the weather improved with warmer temperatures and less snow. April came and I increased my weekly mileage and signed up for a 10K race in Jersey City, New Jersey. Then, on June 15, I got the magical email. I was accepted and now officially training for the 2005 New York City Marathon. Wow!

I got more serious about running by increasing my miles and doing track workouts and hill training. Slowly, at first, I told friends and family. The marathon dream became real. I was ecstatic but nervous. Could I really complete a marathon? As the summer heat became more intense, I increased my mileage from twenty miles per week to thirty, forty, and ultimately peaked at fifty miles per week. I became stronger and more confident. My weekend runs got longer as the time to marathon day got shorter.

When I signed up for the marathon, I had no idea what time I would run it in. I just wanted to be accepted into the race and then figure it out. So, I guessed four hours and wrote that on my application. Then, in September, I ran my first half-marathon in an hour and twenty-nine minutes. Talk about a confidence boost! Look at me, the Olympic athlete! Not only can I run this race, but I bet I can run it in sub-three hours. Boston Marathon, here I come.

The Boston Marathon is one of the few races in America that requires you to qualify for entrance. The prestige, the aura, the "specialness" of Boston is that it requires a challenging qualifying time based on age and gender. Signing up to run a marathon requires a special and committed person. Finishing a marathon is an even more meaningful commitment. Of those very few who actually finish a marathon every year, fewer than five percent qualify to run Boston. This is really an elite pool of runners, and I thought I was one.

Given my age at the time, I needed to run the marathon in less than three hours and ten minutes. Now that I had run a half-marathon in an hour and twenty-nine minutes, I was convinced I could run a Boston-qualifying time. I went to the Jacob Javits Convention Center that Friday in November before the marathon to pick up my race bib and packet. Since I had already submitted my application with a projected four-hour finishing time, my assigned starting corral was with runners projected to finish around four hours. This didn't work for me.

I approached the older woman giving out the race numbers and packets and explained my dilemma. I had conservatively projected a four-hour race time and thus had been given a starting spot with other four-hour runners. But I had run an hour and twenty-nine-minute half-marathon, and I was aiming to break three hours. "Son, I don't know what to tell you," she said. "There is nothing I can do."

I wasn't going to take no for an answer, so I kept prodding. "Surely, you can do something. I am going to run a three-hour marathon, and I can't waste time and energy starting back with the four-hour runners." She clearly didn't respect my athletic prowess (at least in my own mind). As I kept pushing, she said, "Look, you can go to that room over there where the elite club runners check in and see what they can do." She pointed to a door in the corner.

So I took my number and packet and ran over to a small office in the corner of the buzzing Jacob Javits Convention Center. I walked in ready for another battle. A tall, lanky runner-type guy stood behind the counter. I explained my situation, and he said, "Give me your bib." He put a blue ink stamp of the Statue of Liberty on my bib and a green dot sticker. He said this would give me access to the elite running club area at the starting line.

Not knowing what it meant, I showed up at the starting line at the base of the Verrazano Bridge to find a "special" area for elite club runners. I flashed my bib to security and was admitted to the gated section. Separate bathrooms and tables were set up with water bottles and snacks. *Wow, look at me*, I thought. I warmed up and talked to some of the other runners. All were part of elite running clubs, and all had run multiple marathons. Here I was, a first-time marathon runner talking about breaking three hours.

A loudspeaker directed the runners to the start. Among a sea of forty thousand or so runners, I joined other elite club runners about one hundred feet behind the starting line. The world's top-ranked professional runners were merely a few feet ahead of me. I could spit on them if I tried. I didn't try. The cannon shot off, and so did I. I was with the best runners in the world, and I was going to run like an elite runner, even if I wasn't one. As we climbed the Verrazano Bridge at the start, my adrenaline was pumping. I ran my heart out. I felt strong and confident. The first mile came up fast as I ran at a 6:45 mile pace. *Wow, this is going to be easy. I got this.* By the 10K mark, I was averaging 7:04 per mile pace and feeling great.

Remember that Olympic runner I portrayed myself to be? Well, as the miles ticked off, fatigue set in. This fatigue became discomfort, which then became outright pain. By the time I had crossed into Manhattan around mile sixteen, my legs cramped, and every muscle in my body ached. This wasn't passing discomfort, but all-out pain. The sub-three-hour marathon was no longer a realistic goal. Now, finishing was all I could hope for. I trudged up First Avenue as my legs seized. I made a weak, painful smile as I passed my friends and family gathered on First Avenue. I barely shuffled up First Avenue to the Bronx and made the turn back toward Central Park and the finish line. I was running on empty, maybe less than empty.

With wobbly steps and knives of pain piercing my legs, I entered Central Park knowing the finish line was just around the corner. But this late in the race, "around the corner" felt like the other side of the country. I had made it twenty-three-plus miles, and nothing would stop me now. Of course, with every step I also realized I had three more miles to survive. And I mean *survive.*

Just past the twenty-four-mile mark, my body gave out. My right calf muscle seized and cramped so tightly I fell hard to the ground. I could see the calf muscle twisted up and shifted all the way around the right side of my fibula. I didn't know the human body could do that. Yup, it was totally out of place, and I had tears of pain and disappointment streaming down my cheeks. Less than two miles to go, and I was on my hands and knees on the pavement in Central Park. I watched with dismay as dozens of runners passed me. I couldn't get up.

"Are you alright? Can you get up?" another runner said as his hand slapped me on my sweat-soaked back.

I didn't have the energy to turn around and look. I just grunted, "I am cramped and can't get up." I had a flashback of the commercial with the old woman saying, "I have fallen, and I can't get up."

"It's just a cramp. You can do it. You are almost there. Let's go." He took his hand off my back and came around in front. His sweaty legs were inches from my face. I didn't know what he looked like as I could barely lift my head. He hooked his arms under my arms and lifted me up. Salty sweat and tears hit my lips as I barely stood up.

He looked me in the eyes and said, "You aren't quitting now. Let's go finish this together."

I hobbled a few steps and then got into my stride slowly. "We are almost there. We are almost there. We are almost there," he kept repeating. "You have worked so hard and trained, and you are steps from the finish line," he said. We came around the final bend together and saw cones narrowing the road toward the finish line. The bold white "FINISH" jumped off the blue banner marking the finish line. My pain dissipated, and I smiled. I was going to cross that finish line, and this stranger made sure of that.

I had never met him before, and I never saw him again. He probably told me his name when we were limping to the finish line, but I don't recall it. This random act of kindness was one of the greatest gifts I have ever received. When I was down and hurting and doubting, he selflessly slowed his own pace to have a life-altering positive impact on a random stranger. Me!

In the end, I ran a 3:38 that day and didn't qualify for Boston. It took me two more years and two more races to run a Boston-qualifying time in Philadelphia in November of 2007. But that November day in New York, a complete stranger got me across the finish line of my first marathon. Fifteen marathons (three of which were Boston) and one Ironman triathlon later, I am forever grateful to that stranger in Central Park and his random act of kindness.

LITSG believes we have so much happiness to spread around the world, and the most fun way to do it is randomly. Set out each day to make someone else's day a bit better. Surprise adds an amazing element to happiness. Random acts of kindness bestow happiness on the giver and the receiver.

JUST SMILE... IT'S EASY

Smiling may be the easiest of all LITSG behaviors. It takes so little but means so much. Smiling makes us feel good. Think back to how important our first thought of the day is. Now, start each day with a smile. Happiness and smiling are clearly linked. We feel better, and others around us feel better. According to a study published in the *Psychological Bulletin* (Coles, Larson, and Lench 2019), a team of psychologists combined data from 138 studies testing more than eleven thousand participants and concluded that smiling makes people feel happier.

Smiling is a signal to the world about our current state of mind. We are more approachable and vulnerable when smiling. Others are willing to take risks and engage with us when we smile. We feel more confident and happier when we smile. The act of smiling releases brain chemicals that elevate our mood, relax our body, and reduce physical pain. I proactively think about smiling and spend most of my waking minutes smiling. Sometimes my face hurts from smiling so much.

When I am out running, I smile and say hello to everyone I pass. I engage with the local school crossing guards. They always smile back. It is like we are friends. When I walk by a stranger, I often smile, and they almost always smile back. Even in challenging or confrontational situations, a smile is the easiest way to disarm the room and those around you. You would be shocked by how quickly an angry or upset person changes his attitude when you smile at him. It has to be a genuine smile, not a fake one, so get your smile on.

THE POWER OF SYMBOLS

In addition to smiling, I use physical reminders and symbols as triggers to maintain my positive persona. Think about quotes, sayings, and poems. Remember how powerful quotes were to Brianna and Nick Strand. They trigger a positive response. Family pictures serve a similar role. As part of my LITSG philosophy, I use these triggers as activation opportunities.

One trigger I use every day is a poem about happiness and gratefulness. I have it hanging on the bulletin board next to my computer and make sure to read it regularly as a gentle reminder. It is called "If I Knew," and it reminds me that every day can be the last. The poem evokes a thought that we might do things differently and view the world differently if we knew this could be our last day or the last day for someone special in our life. Stop and think about that. If you knew that someone in your life wouldn't be here tomorrow, how would you act differently?

A SHIRT, A SMILE, A BETTER DAY

Small sayings on shirts, mugs, hats—really anywhere—act as symbols and reminders that can make a big difference. Think about the Harvard Model UN T-shirt and how powerful of a symbol it is for me. All of us need reminders. As we get caught in our daily routine, we don't always stop to reflect on our positive self. So how about a mug for your coffee in the morning with a "Just Smile" saying on it? You look at it, and for a fraction of a second, you smile. Already, your day is better.

Recently, at the gym, I saw a woman working out. The woman was not the typical "gym rat" you might expect to see working out. She was wearing a T-shirt and long shorts way past her knees. Her shirt said, "Be Positive." Trying to engage in conversation, I said, "I like your shirt and what it stands for." She smiled and said, "Yeah, I like to wear it as a reminder." In that short interaction, two strangers connected in a positive way over a positive saying. We both smiled. We both felt a positive human interaction. We both were happier than before. A shirt, a smile, and a better day for both of us. LITSG in action.

It takes so little to make a big difference.

Some symbols are temporary reminders. Others are more permanent. Along my LITSG journey, I met Amy Herman, who decided she needed a more permanent symbol as a reminder.

A PERMANENT SYMBOL OF SURVIVAL

No one wants to die alone. Amy Herman wants to make sure of this. "I have a little goal in life. If I can help somebody from not dying alone, I do it."

Amy has had a series of AHA! moments, most recently as a death vigil volunteer. Every Monday, she volunteers at a hospice facility and sits by the bedside of a resident who is actively dying.

"There's always great celebration when people are born. Nobody's born alone. That's by nature. There's always someone in the room when you're born. That's not the case when you die, but there's equal inevitability that we're going to die." Amy understands this as she sits by the bed and holds vigil for those dying.

"What I realized is that you take nothing with you. You go out the way you come in. And it's so interesting, in our world. You see people push and shove achievements and degrees and cars and houses and 401(k)s; none of it goes with you. None of it. It's wonderful that people leave their relatives well taken care of, but when it comes down to us coming into the world and going out, we go out the way we came in."

Spending time by the side of a dying hospice resident reaffirms Amy's commitment to not sweat the small things. She reflects on her conversations with her sister when she leaves her death vigils. Her sister will call and tell her how aggravating work that day was or that her dryer in the laundry room is broken. "And I'm like, you know what, all of that can be fixed. I just came from hospice. And in hospice, we're not trying to solve problems. People are going to die. It's just dealing with the inevitability. I see how dragged down we get by the littlest things and the reason I try not to sweat the little things, honestly, is because I had a near death experience."

Amy's biggest AHA! moment came in 2014. In August of that year, she went for a routine mammogram. The radiologist didn't like what she was seeing and after some further tests, Amy was diagnosed with breast cancer. Shortly thereafter, she met with an oncologist who laid out a plan of treatment. "She tells me I have to do X, Y, Z, A, B, C, and I said I don't really have time for any of that. And she said, 'You need to make the time because in six months, we're not going to be here to discuss it if you don't make the time.' And so, you change your life on a dime because somebody else tells you this is what you have to do."

Amy lost her mother to breast cancer and reflected on the fact that her mother let her fear of cancer overwhelm her will to fight. She died fairly quickly after the diagnosis. Amy wasn't going to be a spectator and let the disease control her. Rather, she took control and did everything she could to beat cancer.

Amy also had earlier AHA! moments in her career. She attended law school and spent five years practicing divorce law before realizing she was wasting time doing something she didn't love. As a part-time docent at the Princeton University Museum of Art, she gave tours on weekends. "I loved when the weekend came because that's when I got to give my tours and my talks, and I thought something is wrong. If you're loving your weekends and hating your weeks, something is definitely wrong. And that's when I sort of had this AHA! moment and started to put the pieces in place."

She built a successful fifteen-year career in art history at various museums including The Brooklyn Museum and The Frick Collection in New York City. During this tenure, Amy developed a program to help medical students improve their observation skills by learning to observe art. This led her to launch and lead her company called The Art of Perception in 2011. She grew her client base to include the New York City Police Department, the Federal Bureau of Investigation, the Department of Justice, and the Secret Service.

In addition to learning not to sweat the small stuff, Amy also had AHA! moments that helped her recognize the power of using symbols and pictures as daily reminders of happiness and gratefulness. In March 2015, she finished chemotherapy, and in April, she had a double mastectomy. She lost her hair, and it was just starting to grow back as stubble when she realized her passport expired. So, in July she went to the post office to get a new passport photo.

She sat in front of the camera, knowing she shouldn't smile for the photo. "What are we frowning about?" the woman behind the camera asked. Amy responded, "Do you want to know the truth? I'm gonna have a passport picture for the next ten years with this reminder of chemotherapy. I have the shortest hair. I almost look bald, and I'm going to have this as my passport picture for the next ten years."

The woman behind the camera told her to sit down and said, "I'm going to tell you about all my close relatives who have passed on because of cancer. I am not only going to take your passport picture; I'm going to take a second picture and I want you to put it in your wallet. And anytime you are feeling sorry for yourself because you have your short hair or you're tired, I want you to remember me and take this picture out of your wallet and say to yourself, *I am alive.*" Amy still carries that picture everywhere with her to this day.

Amy went to an even greater extreme to make sure she had a daily reminder to focus on happiness and gratefulness. Amy's mother attended college with former Supreme Court Justice Ruth Bader Ginsburg. In a twist of fate, Amy had the same cancer team at Memorial Sloan Kettering Hospital as Justice Ginsburg. Amy had Justice Ginsburg's symbolic "dissent collar" tattooed on her chest with the ends of the collar bridging the scar from the port Amy had during chemo—a permanent reminder to keep going.

Amy had numerous AHA! moments in her life. Along the way, Amy learned to not sweat the small stuff, embrace each day, and use symbols as a daily reminder of her happiness and gratefulness. So much of what she learned along her journey exemplifies the LITSG philosophy.

As we learn to live the LITSG philosophy and look for small ways to make a big difference, we can also use music as a positive catalyst.

MUSIC TO MY EARS

I find myself whistling or singing all the time. I whistle so often I taught our pet cockatiel numerous tunes he has been whistling back to me for twenty-five years. I hear a tune or just some random words, and it evokes a song. I usually don't have the words right, but that is irrelevant. Whistling and singing act as a positive release, sometimes to the chagrin of those around me. Even in stressful or difficult situations, whistling or singing helps reduce stress and anxiety and steers us toward a positive, happy attitude.

John Wagstaff, head of the music and performing arts library at the University of Illinois, said whistling is a great form of self-expression and is a wonderful, cheerful activity that lifts one's mood. Wagstaff also notes the broader positive impact whistling has on those around us. When we see or hear others whistling, we want to get involved. Whistling has an infectious positive impact on us.

Singing also makes us happier. Singing releases feel-good chemicals, known as endorphins, into the body. A study published in Australia in 2008 showed that on average, choral singers rated their satisfaction with life higher than the public—even when the actual problems faced by those singers were more substantial than those faced by the general public. A 1998 study found that after nursing home residents took part in a singing program for a month, significant decreases occurred in both anxiety and depression levels. Another study surveying more than six hundred British choral singers found that singing plays a central role in their psychological health.

Whistling and singing are small acts of celebration. Celebrate life. Celebrate happiness. LITSG looks for every chance to celebrate.

AND FINALLY, CELEBRATE!

Every day is an opportunity to celebrate. Small wins add up, and acknowledging success is important to long-term ongoing happiness. Make a big deal about grades, promotions, sports wins, everything and anything. I enjoy celebrating and constantly look for reasons, excuses, and opportunities to celebrate.

At the end of last year, we planned a nice family dinner at a wonderful local steak house. It was December, and everyone was festive and in a holiday mood. I put on my best pair of dark blue jeans, a button-down shirt, and sports jacket, and Jenn and the girls put on beautiful dresses as we went out to celebrate an amazing year and the holiday season. I snuck my iPad into the car and then under my jacket. We parked and trudged our way through the cold, dark, snowy night to the restaurant. The big Christmas tree and Hanukkah menorah were lit and glistening in the town center adjacent to the parking lot. Life was great.

We sat down at the table and after the waiter took our drink order, I reached down under the table to grab my iPad. I was shocked no one noticed when I put it on the floor under my seat.

I took out the iPad, and my daughters had looks of suspicion. "What are you doing, Dad?" I responded, "I am celebrating... life, us, and our successes." I had previously prepared a presentation with one page for each person, plus one page for the family and one page for Jenn and me as a couple.

Each page had a picture showing the highlighted person doing something worth acknowledging. The pages had many bullet points on each. Success is broadly defined to include school promotions, birthdays, anniversaries, volunteer contributions, athletic accomplishments, trips, business successes, hobby growth, and academic accomplishments. The magnitude of the "success" was not relevant. What was most important was the recognition of all the accomplishments. My older daughter Amanda, who was nineteen years old at the time, loved the recognition and smiled from ear to ear as we were celebrating her successes. In her motherly way, Jenn smiled as she watched the girls review the presentation. My younger daughter Jess, who was sixteen years old at the time, just rolled her eyes as if it was goofy. But in a small way, I know she appreciated it.

A few weeks later, we took a family vacation to Cabo. We stayed at a spectacular all-inclusive resort. Each night at dinner, the host or hostess asked if we had any food allergies and if we were celebrating anything. Each time I noted we had no food allergies; however, we were celebrating "life." I then introduced my daughter Jessica as "Life." It was a funny, casual way of celebrating my family and of celebrating life. Some of the servers were entertained by it. For the record, Jess was not entertained and made that clear to me. She laughed and found it funny at first but grew weary of it when I made it a big deal each night at the dinner table. I would point to Jess and say, "We are celebrating life; meet Life!"

As we go through daily life, the cumulative successes we have are not always apparent. Taking the time to acknowledge them, write them out, and celebrate them is a key happiness opportunity and important to the LITSG philosophy.

The LITSG philosophy believes little things make a big difference. Throughout our days, we can constantly look for ways to perform random acts of kindness, smile more, use symbols, and leverage the power of music. More than anything, celebrate. Celebrate success and small wins. Celebrate life, and enjoy each day. Life is too short not to.

1. Smiling, using positive symbols, whistling and singing, random gifts or acts of kindness, and celebrating are all small, easy things we can each do to live a happier and more fulfilling life. Which of these do you proactively do now? Which can you do more of?

2. What are your positive symbols and reminders? How about adding a new one today?

3. What random act of kindness have you performed recently? Look for an opportunity today, tomorrow, and every day to perform a random act of kindness.

4. Celebrating success is so important. Celebrate small successes and make them big celebrations. What can you celebrate and acknowledge as a success today?

CHAPTER 5:

FUNNY THINGS ARE EVERYWHERE

From there to here, from here to there, funny things are everywhere!

—DR. SEUSS,
ONE FISH, TWO FISH, RED FISH, BLUE FISH

Can there possibly be a more powerful statement in American literary history? I mean, c'mon! The brilliant doctor has spoken. My favorite quote in life. It captures the essence of LITSG and the philosophy that humor makes us all happier and makes the world a better place. Reflecting on prior attributes of LITSG, "the power of positivity" and "choose your attitude" are intimately linked to "funny things are everywhere." The trick is finding humor regardless of the situation. Look around, smile, and laugh. It's easy and fun and an important principle of LITSG.

I developed my sense of humor at a young age by spending a lot of time with Poppy. Absolutely nothing was serious about that man. He had amazing energy and found humor everywhere. First, he changed everyone's name. I was Scottso, and my brother Robert was Robare. Not only did humans get nicknames, but inanimate objects also got nicknames. He drove a burnt orange Volkswagen he called Ocho. In fact, he had his own dictionary of names and terms and phrases that my Aunt June created for him. What stuck with me was his ability to look at the world through a lens of humor. He never took himself or the world around him too seriously. He was loud and proud and always looking to have fun. Today, I find humor and fun everywhere, in part because of him.

So why humor? Well, as a starting point, it is a common language. I'm not saying we all find the same things funny. In fact, humor is personal and varies considerably from person to person and culture to culture. However, the ability to approach a person or situation with a sense of humor often makes that situation seem less serious. This disarms people and helps them to open up and embrace the world around them.

In many relationships, people perceive or believe that some person or group has the "upper hand" or a more dominant personality. This puts others on guard as feeling less important or inadequate. The beauty of humor is that it breaks this barrier down. Humor often levels the playing field.

THE EPITOME OF SERIOUSNESS

Nothing seems more serious than a funeral. How about when you are standing next to the open coffin saying your last goodbyes to a loved one?

As I stood by Dad's casket, my phone rang. Many would find this inappropriate, disrespectful, and just plain wrong. Not LITSG. I answered and loudly said, "Hey, Dad, how are you doing? How can I be helpful?" Obviously, it wasn't Dad but rather the rabbi telling me he was running late to the funeral. It didn't matter. I took a challenging situation and turned it on its head and found humor. It made me feel better and happier, and it made those around me more comfortable. I did get some strange looks and reactions, but that is part of my philosophy of not taking the world too seriously.

Let's hang here for a minute on the depressing topic of funerals. Well, to be honest, I find humor at funerals too. Why be stoic in a eulogy? From Mom's eulogy: "Part feline. Yes, I said feline, as in cat. I really believe Mom had at least nine lives, maybe more. She was seriously ill about fifteen years ago, and most didn't think she would make it out of the hospital. She defied medical logic and kept on going. Nothing could kill her. I suspect some people tried."

If you can find and share humor at a funeral, you can find and share humor anywhere and everywhere.

WHAT ABOUT WHEN THEY JUST DON'T LIKE YOU?

I have successfully used humor in the corporate board-room, around the negotiation table, and in litigious mat-ters. Let me pause to clarify that they respected me in the boardroom, but we had serious moments and moments that required hard discussions. At one meeting, a director on my board pressed me hard on my corporate strategy and vision by asking if I had one. Rather than getting into a challenging debate that would have led to a death spiral of negativity, I started my response with, "Not really; I have been winging it all along. Surprised it took you so long to catch on." Everyone laughed, and I explained the strategy. Humor disarmed the room and changed the tone.

Another time I was at the negotiation table having a series of challenging discussions. We got to a point where the other side said there was no way they could give on a point. I pressed "No way?" and they emphasized *"No way."* I pressed one more time and asked, "There is really no fact pattern where you can give this?" and they responded, "I don't think so." This was my window, and I referred to the cinematic masterpiece *Dumb and Dumber* and said, "So you're telling me there's a chance..." and then pumped my fist and yelled "Yeah!" Everyone in the room burst out in laughter, and the tone moving forward was much more cordial.

NOT JUST ONCE, BUT FLAT OUT TWICE

Our daughters' bat mitzvahs were big events for our family. I mean *big*. We love to party, and we were destined to make these epic celebrations. Jenn and I put significant time and energy into making these days particularly special and memorable. And of course, fun. Every detail was carefully thought through and focused on. No detail was too small, and nothing would go wrong. Damn it, I guaranteed it. It would be perfect.

For our older daughter Amanda's bat mitzvah, we prepared a surprise synchronized family dance. Actually, we did it for both bat mitzvahs, but let's focus on Amanda's dance first. We had the dance professionally choreographed, and a dancer taught it to us. The entire family was in on it. I insisted we practice *every* week. Nothing was going to get in our way. This was going to be absolutely perfect.

On the big day, we practiced one final time on the actual dance floor before the guests entered the room. Then, when it was our time, the DJ called Amanda and me onto the dance floor for the traditional daddy/daughter dance. We started like all other similar dances with some sappy song and a slow dance. Then, all of a sudden, the DJ scratched the record and a new, fun, upbeat song blared from the speakers, and we pivoted to our choreographed dance. Jenn and Jess were waiting on the edge of the floor and joined us as the next song came on. Remember, we practiced and practiced and practiced and then... *thud*! Yup, Jenn lost her footing in her "sophisticated" flip-flops and fell flat to the floor. I mean flat. Not a graceful fall, but an all-out flop. *Splat!* It didn't slow any of us down. She didn't miss a beat, and neither did we. We laughed and picked up where we left off, as if it never happened. Rather than letting a possibly negative moment ruin an otherwise perfect day, we just saw the humor and laughed. We still laugh. What a story.

While you might think that is funny (and it was) and give us credit for bouncing back so quickly, wait until you hear what happened two years later. Again, significant focus on details and perfection as we prepared for Jess's bat mitzvah. I was even more fired up for this one since it was our last. It was going to be an even more epic party.

As the party began, Jenn and I waited in the hall as the DJ introduced the family and we entered to music and a cheering crowd. About two hundred people yelled, and the place was fired up. I pressed the DJ on making it the best night ever and coming with more energy than he has ever had. And when I say, "I pressed," I probably crossed the line of pressing to insanity, but he had his marching orders. He later told me he never quite worked with someone like me. I am not sure if it was a compliment or a critique, but it doesn't matter.

The music blasted, the crowd cheered, and energy poured out of me. I jumped up and down in the hallway outside the main room with adrenaline pumping through me. You might've thought I was getting ready to run to the floor of a basketball arena for the national championship. Jenn and I grabbed hands, and the door flew open. We peered into the bright lights and bolted through the tunnel of guests. We raced, jumped, danced, smiled, sang, and… fell! Yup, Jenn and I toppled over and fell flat to the ground. Completely flat.

Some controversy remains to this day about who pulled whom down and whether our dear friend Josh might have impeded our progress or meddled in some way, but it is irrelevant. Video evidence remains inconclusive. Faced for the second time with adversity and a setback, we rolled right through the fall and returned to a vertical position and continued our sprint to the dance floor. We laughed and let the humor carry us through the situation. Life is too short… Life Is Too Short Guy finds humor everywhere.

Humor comes from unique places and situations. My high school buddy Greg Hoyt dealt with an incredibly difficult situation and said he learned the power of humor and laughter to get him through it.

TAKING IT LESS SERIOUSLY…
A CHANGE IN PERSPECTIVE

"This is the moment when you start living, rather than waiting around… waiting for life to come to you… which is, let's make memories," said Greg.

Campbell "Cam" Hoyt was a happy, talkative three-year-old when her parents noticed a small slur in her voice. Nothing too abnormal; she just sounded like maybe "she had a couple too many glasses of wine." Then, her parents, Greg and Robin, noticed her balance was a bit off. Once she started running a fever, they took her to a pediatrician to find out what was wrong. Multiple doctors ran tests to diagnose her, without success. She was tested for strep, the flu, mono, and even Lyme disease. Greg and Robin decided to take matters into their own hands and turned to Dr. Google yet still couldn't figure it out.

They then met a physician who quickly knew something wasn't quite right. He saw Cam and said, "I'm going to send you to Morristown Medical Center, and I want them to do a CAT scan. You know, I'm not ready to introduce you to my wife yet, but I want you to have a CAT scan first... just to rule some things out."

This matter-of-fact statement raised Greg's antenna. He asked, "So what does your wife do?"

The doctor responded, "Oh, she's a pediatric oncologist."

On August 20, 2009, Greg, Robin, and Cam drove to Morristown Medical Center for a CAT scan. They didn't get to perform the scan until late in the evening. Robin and Greg were anxiously awaiting the results in the emergency room while Cam was lying there perfectly happy when two doctors walked in. Greg knew having two doctors deliver the results was an ominous sign—the first of many to come.

"And they came in and they said—and I'll never forget the words they used—'We saw something we didn't want to see.' Then we said, 'Okay, what did you see?' to which the doctors responded, 'She has a massive brain tumor at the base of her brain. It's likely cancerous. The neurosurgeon is on her way in.'"

Greg's initial reaction was complete numbness. He equated the feeling to being hit by a ton of bricks. It took Greg and Robin a few minutes to absorb the news and begin to comprehend what it meant. Just then, their pediatrician showed up in the room. The doctors had called her with the results, and she had driven to the hospital, arriving around midnight.

Cam was transferred from the ER to the pediatric intensive care unit to prepare for surgery two days later. In just over forty-eight hours, life for the Hoyt family completely turned upside down. Life as they knew it would never be the same. The next two days were particularly challenging. "Watching a three-year-old go in for surgery is hard. She was miserable. They came up, the whole neurosurgery team comes up, and they just allowed us to carry her down to the OR, which was relatively unusual. Just walk her down. Because she was scared, of course. She went in for surgery for six or seven hours while they removed the tumor. Then they brought her up with a million tubes, and she was on a ventilator. She had IVs everywhere."

This was just the beginning of a long and arduous journey for the Hoyt family. Shortly after, Cam returned to the hospital for another brain surgery to stop the leaking of spinal fluid caused by the first surgery. Then, she battled meningitis for six months. The inability to find the source of the meningitis led to another brain surgery. While battling all the setbacks thrown at her, Cam remained cancer-free for eleven months.

But the cancer returned—first on one part of her spine and then on other parts. She endured numerous rounds of radiation and chemotherapy. By the time she was five, she had already received her lifetime dose of radiation.

As 2013 came to a close, the cancer was progressing and Cam was struggling. Greg and Robin were trying to "outrace" the cancer but knew something just wasn't right. Her eyes weren't working properly, and her personality started to change. She had surgeries in January, April, and June to remove three different tumors. The June surgery was a particularly challenging one. Cam's health was rapidly declining.

Prior to the June surgery, they were presented with a very difficult decision about having the surgery. As Greg recalls, "We're in the intensive care at Sloan Kettering with the neurosurgeon and the pediatric neuro oncologist—both super-talented doctors and just good people, generally caring people. And they were both visibly shaken, and they said, 'You know, we can do this, but we kind of have two choices.' They explained that we can either let nature take its course or we can do another surgery and maybe buy ourselves a few months." So, they turned to Campbell, who was eight at this time and asked her if she wanted to have the surgery. She said she did, and thus they progressed with the surgery.

Cam declined rapidly in the weeks after the surgery, losing her ability to walk and talk. On a Sunday in late August, she had a massive seizure and was never conscious again. With her family around her, she passed away a few days later on August 21, 2014. This was exactly five years and one day from her cancer diagnosis. By pediatric cancer standards, Cam was a positive statistic. A survivor.

Greg had a series of AHA! moments over the five years Cam battled cancer. His perspective changed immensely. "While losing her was extremely negative, what's come out of it for my wife and me and our family is this tremendous gift of perspective. So that when things are going sideways, look, it can always be worse. There's always somebody who has it worse than you do. So, count your blessings."

The most poignant AHA! moment for Greg came when, after eleven months of being cancer-free and believing they beat it, the cancer returned for the first time. "This is the moment when you start living, rather than waiting around... waiting for life to come to you... Let's make memories." And that is what the Hoyt family did. They embraced their time together, traveled, and shared special experiences.

The Hoyt family also learned to focus on small things and to find humor and reasons to celebrate. "Just making light of the things that happen along the way and living in that moment and finding the joy in the little moments, even in an otherwise very unfortunate situation. Laughing at the jokes she made about losing her own hair and things like that. Her waking up without any clothes on and finding that very strange. The outcome isn't always what we want, but if you can, take advantage of those little moments. We still talk about them today."

Weeks before Cam would have turned sixteen, Greg reflected on the key lessons his family learned from this AHA! moment. "We see things a little bit differently. And we don't necessarily take things as seriously as we did before. And little things don't tend to derail us as much as they would have before. The second thing would be taking advantage of the time we have and being present. And then, I think that the other would be understanding the value of giving back."

Greg and Robin founded the Team Campbell Foundation to fund research to end childhood cancers, to provide financial support for families dealing with childhood cancers, and to sponsor bereaved parent trips for parents who have lost a child to cancer. The desire to give back was inspired by Cam herself. For her sixth birthday, instead of a party, she organized a bake sale with her friends and raised five thousand dollars. She told her parents she wanted to raise money "to help kids like me."

While Greg learned later in life the importance of humor and laughter, Brendan Murray discovered it while struggling to make ends meet and put food on his table in college.

LAUGH WHEN YOU HIT THE BOTTOM

"I was four foot, eight inches when I started high school. That's the size of most people in fourth grade. I was first in line at graduation because I was the shortest and we went in height order," Brendan Murray recalls. "I didn't fit in well." That belief continued when college started until one night at a fraternity house foosball table.

Brendan is a close friend I asked to share his life experiences. He didn't have it easy growing up. His parents were divorced, and he worked hard to support himself. The summer before college, he worked days on a construction site and nights on the Jersey Shore boardwalk. Days could start at 7 a.m. and end the next morning at 2 a.m. As he was getting ready to head off to freshman year at the University of Delaware, he found out his father wasn't going to pay for college as he had expected. He planned to be roommates with his high school friend, but that all changed, and a last-minute pivot led him to Rutgers University.

During his freshman year, the challenges continued. Brendan's roommate was a senior and his dorm was on a quieter, isolated campus. He never really embraced college life and considered leaving. Then, a few weeks into his sophomore year, Brendan was "dragged" to a fraternity house for a rush party. The foosball table called, and he answered. Brendan had played a lot of foosball as a kid and was pretty good at it. Who wouldn't answer the call of a foosball table?

At this table Brendan had his AHA! moment. The fraternity house was playing "winners stay." He said, "I got on that foosball table and never left. I met every single person because I was stationary. And I had no intention of joining something like that. I just jumped in with both feet, and it really formed a lot of my future friendships for my life. It gave me a confidence that I didn't have before, and it made me a completely different person."

In the pre-foosball table life, Brendan hadn't enjoyed high school or college. At "The Table" he found himself and had the realization it was time to live life and have fun.

Shortly thereafter, he found himself and his newfound friends on a "pledge trip," randomly heading south to nowhere. "We rented a van, threw two mattresses in the back, and drove south. I mean, it was eight guys, and we barely had enough money to make it on this trip."

The "road trip" of college had many twists and turns. One such twist was when, in his junior year, Brendan realized he was down to his last five dollars during winter break. He had to make a calculated decision of what to do with that last five dollars. He debated whether to buy a tank of gas and drive to his mom's house or to buy himself peanut butter, jelly, and a loaf of bread, figuring he could survive for a few weeks on PB&J sandwiches. He decided on the PB&J, but it didn't work out exactly as planned.

"I came home and put the peanut butter and jelly in the refrigerator. I put the loaf of bread on top, and I'm sitting there watching television and all of a sudden, the bread is moving across the top of the refrigerator. I go over to pick it up, and the whole side of it is eaten out by the mice that were dragging it across the top of the refrigerator because they were hungry too. I ate peanut butter and jelly with a spoon for three weeks until school started again, and the kitchen reopened."

Brendan laughed as he remembered the story. He reflected on the fact that even at what seemed like the worst of times, he just had to laugh and see the humor in it. As he watched the bread being dragged away by mice, he had a major AHA! moment that led him to his perspective on humor and laughter. He says he uses humor and laughter today as a guiding light to help him navigate life.

FIND HUMOR, AND TAKE LIFE LESS SERIOUSLY

LITSG strongly believes that humor and laughter ground us in a happier, more fulfilling life. Studies have shown that funny people tend to be smarter, healthier, and less stressed about life. According to an article published in *The Insider* in 2017, funny people tend to appear more attractive to romantic partners, funny bosses lead better teams, and funny teachers create stronger students. Not only do funny people make others laugh, but they also laugh more themselves. Further evidence suggests that humor boosts perceptions of confidence, competence, and status, enhancing the influence of funny people (Bitterly 2016). As we think about the key principles of LITSG, "the power of positivity," and "choose your attitude," it is clear how important humor is to LITSG and living a happier, more fulfilling life.

You have the opportunity to find humor everywhere and in every situation. Don't take yourself, your situation, or life too seriously. Smile, laugh, and embrace it. And as the great Dr. Seuss told us, funny things are everywhere.

LITSG REFLECTIONS

1. Humor breaks down barriers and generally welcomes people into a social situation. When have you used humor to welcome others in? How can you use humor to expand your social influence?

2. Humor works in all situations if you have the right attitude. Think about a time you were in a difficult situation when humor may have been a good tool to defuse the stress and pressure. Look for new opportunities today to interject humor in awkward or uncomfortable situations.

3. Laughing makes people feel happier. How often during the day do you find yourself laughing? How often do you find yourself making others laugh? Become a proactive laugher and a laugh-creator today.

4. Humor is an outlet for stress and negative emotions. Can you think of times when you used humor as a stress reliever? How about today?

CHAPTER 6:

TICK, TICK... BOOM— MINUTES MATTER

A man who dares to waste one hour of life has not discovered the value of life.

—CHARLES DARWIN

No one has ever accused me of being patient. Note how I use the word "accuse," as if patience is a bad thing. And according to my LITSG philosophy, it is! As I discussed earlier, at birth we each have approximately forty-two million projected minutes in our lives. Depending on where you are on the life curve, you probably have substantially fewer minutes left. I value each moment and look for ways to maximize these minutes. I call it "positive urgency," and the LITSG principle is "minutes matter."

Certain circumstances require some level of waiting or delay of gratification. I approach these situations with skepticism and as opportunities to think differently. I do a bit of mental math and think about the "investment" of time that patience requires and what the reward or payoff is. I look at how I am using my minutes and assess delayed gratification and I ask:

1. Is it worth it? This activity requires me to invest time either by waiting or delaying or spending time. What is the reward?

2. Can I find creative ways to shorten the delay? We often can, but we don't proactively look for them. We just accept the norm. Stop accepting and start questioning.

3. Can I find ways to enhance the reward for waiting? If I am going to wait, how can I get a better return for waiting?

4. Is there a compromise where I can get greater value for less investment of time?

5. Is there something I can do at the same time as I have to wait to get an unrelated return? For example, can I make new friends while standing in line? Can I send a note to a friend while I am waiting for an appointment?

LET'S SEE HOW FAST I CAN GET IT DONE

I can do it faster than you! Maybe not always, but that is my mindset. I look for ways to shorten the path to accomplish things quicker than expected. This is how I make the most of the limited minutes in my life.

I started down this path when I was young. I joined the Boy Scouts when I was eleven years old. The Boy Scouts provide a very clear path for advancement and recognition as scouts learn new skills and earn merit badges to climb the Boy Scout ladder. It is hierarchical and prescriptive. A scout must earn twenty-one merit badges and advance through seven distinct and clearly defined scouting ranks to reach the top of the ladder: Eagle Scout.

In the 1980s, when I was a Boy Scout, according to *On Scouting Magazine* (Wendell 2015), only about 1.3 percent of all scouts made it to the rank of Eagle Scout. The average age of attaining the rank of Eagle Scout is approximately seventeen years old. I embraced the challenge at eleven years old and looked for a faster way. To achieve my goal, I attended Boy Scout camp each summer and took extra merit badge classes early in the morning (like bird watching) and late in the evening (like astronomy). For three years, I earned six merit badges per summer. In 1988, I reached the rank of Eagle Scout at fourteen and a half years old. At the time, I was among the youngest to have ever achieved the rank.

It is logical to ask if I gave up some benefits by moving so quickly. No doubt, the answer is yes. We gain a greater level of maturity and appreciation for the rank and the skills learned along the way by taking a slower path. However, even then, I did my analysis and asked the questions above. I decided the benefit of achieving the Eagle Scout rank sooner outweighed the tradeoffs. This is a choice each person needs to make. LITSG merely prescribes that we deliberately make that assessment. How am I spending each of my precious minutes, and can I spend each one better?

Let me give you another example. I went to college without a clear plan of exactly what I wanted to study or what I wanted to do after college. I had a rough idea I might explore law school. Upon starting college at Rutgers, I stumbled across a joint BA/MBA program mentioned in the academic catalog. I discovered I could complete both my BA and MBA in five years by sharing the credits earned during my first year of graduate study with my undergraduate credit requirements. Then, as I explored further, I discovered separately, an accelerated and intensive fifteen-month MBA program.

The traditional MBA path was two years and included a fall and spring semester each of the two years. The accelerated program jammed four semesters into fifteen months. It started in May and finished in August the subsequent year. So, I inquired about using the accelerated BA/MBA template and substituting in the fifteen-month MBA so both degrees could be completed in just over four years.

I walked into the Rutgers dean's office with the course catalog and waited to speak to someone. I tried to explain what I was looking to do, but no one had done this before, and they weren't exactly sure how to make it happen logistically.

After waiting a bit, I finally met with a dean who rattled off a long list of questions neither of us could answer. What tuition would I pay to what department during what semester? Would I be eligible for undergraduate housing while pursuing a graduate degree, but before graduating undergraduate? Large institutions aren't built to think differently. The LITSG philosophy compels us to think differently. In this case, I was thinking about the fastest, most efficient route to complete my academic work. Minutes matter, and I didn't want to use too many up in stuffy classrooms.

I finished three years of full-time undergraduate education at the end of the spring semester in May of 1994. A few weeks later, I began my graduate studies and continued full time through the summer, fall, spring, and summer semesters, completing two years of graduate business school in fifteen months and only three months beyond when I would have traditionally finished undergraduate studies. So rather than just completing my BA in May of 1995, I completed both my BA and MBA by August of 1995.

Again, there were tradeoffs. I was young and immature and didn't capture some of the nuances that mature students bring to business school. I remember our tax professor offered to take the class for drinks on the first day of class, and I wasn't even twenty-one years old. But as I reflect on this over twenty-five years later, it didn't matter. What really mattered is I had finished both my BA and MBA before my twenty-second birthday, and I was ready to enter the business world and start the next challenge. By shaving off almost two years of a traditional BA and MBA path, I banked about a million minutes I could use elsewhere.

The next challenge was starting my career as an entry-level accountant at PricewaterhouseCoopers. Large accounting firms also have well-worn paths to advancement. The proverbial ladder. Like in both the Boy Scouts and academia, they have a hierarchal and prescriptive structure. You start as an auditor and work three years to become a senior auditor and then on to manager, etc. But I didn't buy into the predetermined path. Again, I applied my LITSG philosophy that minutes matter. So why waste any?

The first thing I discovered was that almost everyone followed the traditional advancement path and assumed it was the only way. Why try to distinguish yourself if you are part of a class that will progress together up the ranks? As a young auditor, I discovered that the key was to make life easier for my supervisor. If I could make my supervisor look good, I would develop a positive reputation and attract attention from others around the firm. And that is exactly what I did.

I was given a time budget for completing every task. For example, twenty hours to reconcile cash accounts, thirty hours to test accounts receivable, etc. It seemed these budgets were established over many years of precedent and each generation of new accountants worked to deliver the product in the prescribed time. However, if I worked hard, stayed focused, and continued to challenge myself, I could perform most tasks in considerably less time than budgeted. This made my manager look really good, which helped her develop a positive reputation. As a result of this early epiphany, I was able to work with key partners on important projects and was promoted one year early. Rather than the standard three-year path to senior auditor,

I was promoted in two years. By shaving off a year of the traditional path to promotion, I banked another half million minutes. Wow, the banked minutes were adding up!

Minutes matter. It's that simple. And I use this mantra in everything I do, big and small. It is who I am, and how I operate. As an example, buying and selling real estate is a complicated process. Commercial real estate is even more complicated and time consuming as you go through the diligence and legal process. Transactions typically take months, maybe years. I recently worked with a veteran real estate lawyer named Mark who said to me, "You are the only person I have ever worked with on a real estate transaction who said, 'Minutes matter.'"

In order to make the most of my finite minutes, the LITSG philosophy is built on the power of goal setting. Without goals, it is hard to know how to use your minutes wisely. You need to define your direction and path.

GOAL SETTING... A ROADMAP TO MAXIMIZING MINUTES

Each day is a new day, a new beginning, a new opportunity. Each day uses up approximately 1,400 of my finite and precious minutes. How do I maximize the value of these minutes? I start by preparing for each day the prior day. Each evening I write a list of goals for the next day and arrange them in the order in which I plan to accomplish them. This is my roadmap. I consider priorities, time to completion, physical challenges (e.g., locations), and other factors as I create the order.

Written goals are important to preparing for each day. The format is not relevant. Find a place where you can quickly scratch out goals. Do it the day before. Make them as simple as possible. Don't waste time overthinking. Just capture them in written form and prioritize them.

The ability to see written goals creates a framework that makes them real. Saying "I want to... tomorrow" makes the goal nebulous, a theory, a wish. Recording them makes it real and actionable. As the day progresses and goals are accomplished, I love to cross them off. We experience a positive psychological effect to seeing success by crossing off individual goals. At the end of the day, I reflect on my daily accomplishments. Regardless of what it is, I find success. I define success for the day by what I completed, rather than what is uncompleted. Focus on the positive, not the negative. I then move the uncompleted goals to the next day and add new goals. The list is never complete, but progress is made.

Goals are the cornerstone to a life well-lived. I acknowledge that sometimes the greatest happiness comes from spontaneity. This should not be ignored. But too many minutes are wasted without a plan, and this is what LITSG tries to avoid.

Goals help create a broad roadmap to show a path from here to there. It helps us define our purpose. In addition to the daily goals discussed above, I live in a Goals Grid. My Goals Grid is set up with four columns and four rows. The rows are labeled Personal, Family, Professional, and Physical. The columns are labeled Daily, Monthly, Annually, and Longer. Longer can be further segmented into more specific timelines (two-year, five-year, ten-year, etc.). Timelines create accountability. The grid creates a pictorial description of where you want to go and over what timeline. The more you can put on the grid, the better.

THE GOALS GRID

	Daily	Monthly	Annually	Longer
Personal				
Family				
Professional				
Physical				

Be realistic, but stretch. Think about a broad range of goals, and clearly define them. This may include travel goals, physical challenge goals, happiness goals, career goals, relationship goals, or anything else you want to accomplish. But until you write them down and define a timeline, goals remain abstract. Once you put goals on the grid, it becomes a path to accomplishment and a grid of accountability. These rows and columns help set the tone for priorities, timelines, and areas of focus. Personal goals come first as a priority. Taking care of oneself is the most important so you have the ability to take care of your family and your business. The grid is a malleable tool, and each person should adapt it based on personal preference. Most importantly, create your grid today and set regular reminders to revisit and update your grid as priorities change.

PRIORITIES MATTER TO LITSG

If you only had one day left, what would you do with it? By definition, having a finite number of minutes to work with means we each have to prioritize. Being proactive and setting those priorities on a regular basis are important. No one should set your priorities. We each have to decide what is most important for our finite set of minutes and use our minutes wisely. Don't just throw minutes away without thinking how best to use them to achieve your goals.

Imagine a barrel of minutes and every time you remove one, fewer remain in the barrel. Be careful of leaks in this barrel. Don't lose minutes without knowing where they are going. Understand that you can't replenish minutes. Eventually, the barrel is empty. Your ability to dream and create a Goals Grid helps you define your priorities. Realize, these priorities will change over time, or they can change in an instant.

PIVOT MOMENTS

We have seminal moments in life when we each have the opportunity to pivot in a meaningful way. This pivot could be related to work, hobbies, family, friends, or just about anything. Pivots are changes in course. We were on this road historically, and now we are taking a new road to the future. The pivot may be massive or minor, but it does change the current direction, with implications for the future. Priorities change, and thus goals change.

Pivots can be voluntary or involuntary. For example, I made a voluntary pivot when I left a Wall Street corporate job to join an entrepreneurial start-up. An example of an involuntary pivot is when someone loses a spouse or partner and begins a new life without that loved one. To a certain degree, the pivot is still voluntary in terms of choosing the path forward, but the involuntary nature of the event causing the pivot changes the dynamic.

Make the most of pivots. Like each new day, pivots provide an opportunity to reset expectations, attitudes, goals, and priorities. In so many of my life experiences, I learned from and made the most of pivots. On September 11, 2001, I had a major AHA! moment that added accelerants to my "minutes matter" mantra.

IT'S FAMILY TIME

The sun was shining brightly on this beautiful fall Tuesday. I woke up after another short night of sleep and headed back to the office for an early call with a potential client in Japan. This was life as a junior investment banker.

I walked out the door of my Hoboken condo and turned on Newark Street on my way to the downtown ferry terminal. I wasn't the only one heading to work as dozens of others were walking at a hurried pace. It was about seventy degrees Fahrenheit and there wasn't a cloud in the sky. I put on my sunglasses to cut the glare. I passed a Dunkin' Donuts as the sweet smell of fried pastry wafted in the air.

After a seven-minute walk, I hopped on the ferry and enjoyed the five-minute ride into lower Manhattan. It was one of the moments of the day when I just took it in and observed the world around me. What a great way to commute and start the day. The ferry bounced on the small waves as we crossed the Hudson River. I walked past the World Trade Center shortly before 8 a.m. not realizing it would be the last time I would walk by the towers. The world I knew was about to change forever.

I entered the building at 388 Greenwich Street in lower Manhattan and grabbed a quick breakfast in the cafeteria. I then took the elevator to the thirty-second floor and returned to the cubicle I had vacated just a few hours earlier. Given the number of late nights and early mornings, the days often blended. Maybe I had left minutes ago—who knew? A quick check of my email, and off to an office to hop on the call.

It was an exploratory call with a global healthcare company. I had participated in many of these. I spent the night before preparing M&A ideas for the prospective client to consider. After getting the standard pleasantries out of the way, the pitch began. This one was no different, until it was.

Just over fifteen minutes into the call, a loud bang made me jump—an explosion of some sort. It was loud enough to draw attention but far enough away that it didn't raise any alarm. The call continued, and I looked out toward the Hudson River and New Jersey, where emergency vehicles raced down the West Side Highway. Not unusual at first, but the flow of vehicles increased. Police cars, ambulances, and fire trucks with flashing lights and wailing sirens passed below with a clear sense of urgency.

We asked our prospective client in Japan if we could take a short break to see what was going on. I pressed the mute button on the speaker phone and headed to the south side of the building. My stomach lurched when I joined others at the window. Thick black smoke billowed from a hole in the side of one of the towers at the World Trade Center. Viewing it from the thirty-second floor of an office about eight blocks north of the World Trade Center, it was difficult to assess the magnitude of the hole.

About a dozen people had now gathered near me, and we all stared at the hole in the side of the World Trade Center without a clue as to how it got there, what it meant, or what else might be coming. The team returned to the call and suggested that we reschedule it so that we could determine what was going on at the World Trade Center.

We returned to the south side of the building, staring through the window with mouths wide open. I grabbed a radio out of my desk and flipped between Bloomberg Radio and the news station 1010 AM. Preliminary reports were that a plane hit the South Tower of the World Trade Center. I heard a hushed whisper as the bankers listened to the radio and stared at the smoldering building. The radio announcers speculated it was a small private plane and probably an accident.

I called Jenn at her office in midtown Manhattan. It was too early to comprehend the magnitude of the events, but I wanted to make sure she knew about the crash. She said she was watching the news coverage on television. I had real concerns, but Jenn didn't. Midtown Manhattan might as well have been in another state. Not seeing it unfolding live out her window, she was considerably less worried. We spoke briefly, and I returned to the window.

Just moments later, a full-sized commercial airplane, flying low, tilted at an angle, circled from across the Hudson River and careened into the second tower. Glass shattered. A massively bright fire ball exploded. This moment and image changed my life forever.

Black smoke poured out of both towers now. Was this real? What was going on? I grabbed my computer, Blackberry, and belongings and hurried to the elevator. I tried calling Jenn again, but the networks were all busy. Elevator or stairs? Time was of the essence, and getting out of the building was my top priority. So, the elevator it would be.

The elevator door opened to a dozen or so alarmed faces. In hushed voices, they worried about friends and family as the elevator sank to the ground floor. The doors opened, and I stepped into chaos in the lobby. Everyone was running for the exits and talking quietly while staring at the ground. No one made eye contact. I ran through the doors and joined hundreds of others racing away from the building as a cacophony of sirens grew louder and louder. Turning to the west, I walked about two hundred yards to the West Side Highway and debated what was the best move.

To the south just a few blocks away, black smoke filled the sky. Much to my surprise, hundreds—maybe thousands—of people were walking south *toward* the World Trade Center. Puzzled by this, I walked north on the West Side Highway to get away from downtown. A black livery car was parked on the side of the road with the driver in it, and the passenger window open. I asked the driver if he could take me north.

"Hop in," he said.

I jumped in the car, my heart racing. "I really want to get out of town quickly. What do you think?"

The driver suggested heading to the midtown piers and seeing what options were available. Fewer than ten minutes and twenty dollars later, I was in the terminal and buying a ticket to take a Circle Line Ferry across the river to Weehawken. It may have been one of the last tickets sold that day before the mass exodus began. Not knowing exactly where I would end up, I just wanted to get out of the city fast.

As the ferry crossed the Hudson, the passengers talked about planes hitting the Pentagon and the White House. No one knew what to believe or what to expect. The United States was under attack. I got off the ferry and looked downtown as the first of the towers to fall that day came crashing down. I hailed a taxi to get back home to Hoboken. Mobile phones were down, and it was difficult for me to reach Jenn. It was getting very scary.

The ten- or fifteen-minute trip to Hoboken felt like a lifetime. Upon arriving home, I ran to my computer and sent an email to a handful of people telling them I was okay. This was long before social media and instant communication. From the rooftop deck I gazed across the Hudson as the remaining tower burned. A thick, putrid, sharp smell of death and fear filled the air. Moments later the second tower crumbled like a Lego set. These two horrifying hours changed my life, my priorities, and my perspective forever. This was another major AHA! moment and a key building block to LITSG.

The ensuing days were quiet and unsettling. Living in Hoboken, only about two miles from Ground Zero, made it even more eerie. The smoke and burning smell hung in the air for weeks. No one knew what to expect, how to behave, or what to do. Hoboken was particularly hard hit as most of the town commuted to Manhattan. The days were long and quiet. The world had ground to a halt.

Less than a month later, Jenn and I boarded a flight to Chicago with great trepidation. It was unsettling to fly again, but we had a wedding to attend and weren't going to miss it. Perhaps more than ever, I felt that life is too short to let fear get in the way of having fun and enjoying life and celebrations.

We arrived in Chicago and attended the wedding of our close friends Amy and Jeff the next day. On this first weekend in October, I sat next to Jenn in a small quiet corner of a quaint room at a beautiful private school. The room was wood paneled and dimly lit. Soft music played and mixed with the sound of clinking glasses in the background. With the cocktail reception going on, the quintessential "life is too short" moment happened, and we agreed to start a family.

My mantra that "minutes matter" suddenly became even more real and accelerated. Only weeks earlier, I was convinced that climbing the investment banking ladder was my highest priority and having children was a nice idea for the future. Maybe someday. Living through a day of death and destruction less than one mile from my office and two miles from my home, I reprioritized my life. Just over one year later, our daughter Amanda was born.

Sometimes, it takes a major near-death AHA! moment for people to first realize minutes matter. For me, 9/11 was an accelerant to my already well-appreciated philosophy about urgency. However, for Barbara, a licensed clinical social worker, she first learned about the importance of setting goals and making the most of her minutes after a suicide attempt.

SHE JUST WANTED TO BE DEAD

"It's not about finding happiness but creating it."

Having two teenage daughters of my own, I know how hard life can be for teenage girls. In a world of intense scrutiny, instant gratification, and social media pressure, it can be a real pressure cooker for teenagers in general and even more so for girls. Teenage years are challenging.

As a freshman in college at the age of eighteen, Barbara had enough. She made a conscious decision to end it all and swallowed about three hundred pills of Tylenol. Much to her chagrin, she survived. Her family rushed to her side and forced her to leave school and seek treatment. Barbara just wasn't in the right mental frame of mind to stay alive. "My parents told me you can't go to school right now. You have to get treatment. And I was pissed off at everyone because they made me stop doing what I was doing. And because I didn't get to choose the treatment. I didn't get to choose the route. Everything was out of my control. And I was already having issues with not being happy in my life and where am I going with this? I didn't want to get better. I just wanted to be dead."

After the near-death experience, Barbara slogged along for three years working various jobs and going in and out of treatment programs. Then her AHA! moment came one day on the job as a customer service representative at Home Depot. "This customer is yelling at me, and I'm like, 'I can't do this anymore. I can't be treated poorly when I'm doing a good job.' Because it wasn't my fault. I have so much more to offer the world. And that was actually a moment where I was like, 'Something's going to be different.' So, I think it was the combined feeling of not being in control and knowing I had so much more to offer."

At that moment, the lightbulb went off for Barbara. She harkened back to a quote she saw while in treatment. "It's not about finding happiness but creating it." As she was dealing with an irate customer, Barbara had a bit of an out-of-body experience. She saw the quote and realized she had to take control and change her life. "I think that up until that moment, I had been just expecting I was going to wake up one day and be happy like that. It's just going to happen overnight. It's just going to fall in your lap. That's not accurate. And so, at that moment, that's when I decided to do something different immediately."

A few weeks later Barbara re-enrolled in college and started on an academic path to a career in counseling. She realized she could create her own story and help others create theirs. Barbara completed her undergraduate degree in social work and psychology before going on to complete her master of social work. She started her own practice as a licensed clinical social worker with a focus on child therapy. She grew the business and built a successful practice. Her biggest takeaway from this AHA! moment was the importance of setting goals. "I think the key was definitely starting to set goals. I hadn't set any goals. I think I was so ready to check out of the world that there was no purpose for a goal. If you're going to go, why would you set a goal? You're not going to achieve it. And then I started setting goals, and that changed everything." Then, her second AHA! moment came along.

In April 2020, Barbara was diagnosed with pneumonia. The original diagnosis developed into an undiagnosed neurological condition that Barbara battles to this day. She deals with seizures and losing control of parts of her body at times. This second AHA! moment really made Barbara stop and reflect on where she was in her life as well as where she was going. Now in her early thirties, she realizes life won't last forever and time is precious. "I don't know if one day I'll just die, or what tomorrow is going to look like. Since then I have spent more time with my family. That became a priority for me."

Barbara has also focused on her professional goals more acutely. She hired three therapists to work for her and is looking to hire more. She built out and renovated additional office space with the hope and expectation that her practice will grow. She is even considering returning to school for a PhD. It took Barbara two major life-altering AHA! moments to realize the need to take control of her life, set goals, and focus on happiness today, because tomorrow isn't guaranteed. She realizes minutes really do matter and wants to make the most of her time. She has set bigger goals and is chasing her dreams.

JUST DREAM

At times, we can be our own biggest obstacle to success and happiness. As we think about setting goals, we have to dream. We each have expectations for what is possible and then we start to dream. We dream small at first and then we are encouraged to dream big. Why quantify dreaming? What is "big"? Can it be bigger? Can it be huge? Quantifying sets an expectation.

You may have a large accomplishment in mind, but there are no parameters to dreaming for LITSG. As you think about creating goals and how to use your minutes wisely, dream, dream, dream. Words like "reasonable," "normal," "historical," and "expected" are irrelevant and limiting. Ignore them. They don't matter. I love to hear "You are crazy" or "You are different" or "Wow, do you really think you can do that?" I encourage you to get out of your own way and don't limit your dreams. Sprinkle goals across the Goals Grid that are wild dreams. You only have a chance of accomplishing what you set out to accomplish. Dream, set goals, and go!

LITSG REFLECTIONS

1. Minutes matter. Even in the most hierarchical and structured organizations, a shortcut or faster path usually exists. Have you ever looked for that shortcut? As you look at your current goals and activities, which will lend themselves to finding a way to use your minutes more efficiently?

2. Did you set goals for today? Do you have weekly, monthly, and annual goals? Reflect and revise your existing goals today. Set new goals today. Minutes matter; don't wait until tomorrow.

3. What was the last major pivot moment in your life? How did you deal with it? What positive came from it?

4. What does the word "dream" mean to you? Close your eyes and just dream. Eliminate all preconceived notions of reality and dream. Ignore impossibility. Write those dreams down. Set goals to make them happen.

CHAPTER 7:

LEARN, LEARN, LEARN

Live as if you were to die tomorrow. Learn as if you were to live forever.

—MAHATMA GANDHI

"Why are you in this class today?" the instructor asked. He was clearly fired up and excited to be there. He had just reviewed the long list of rules for the class. I sat in the classroom stunned and thinking, *I am forty-eight years old and the CEO of a public company, and I am being told if I am late coming back from the breaks, I won't be admitted to the classroom and I can call my parents to pick me up.* It was the beginning of an all-day marathon session in a windowless conference room in a rundown hotel in the middle of nowhere. Who would want to be sitting there? About half the participants were teenagers and the other half looked like they were there with a teenaged son or daughter.

"For the money! I hear it is really good money," said the young teenager next to me. I looked at him and said, "Yeah, me too. I am in it for the money." I tried hard not to laugh as I reflected on why I was there. This was soccer referee training. I grew up playing soccer as a child and continued playing as an adult. I coached both of my daughters' teams and loved it. I am enamored with soccer and wanted to be around it more. So, I decided it was time to learn something new. I signed up to become a referee.

First, it was online training, then in the classroom, and finally on the field. As a spectator and player, it seemed easy. Wow was I wrong. But it was fun and intellectually stimulating to learn an entirely new set of skills. I had to hone my knowledge of the rules and then learn practical applications, game management, and how to deal with a lot of crazy, angry parents and coaches. Sadly, I used to be one of them.

So why did I do it? I did it entirely for the learning experience and the opportunity to challenge myself. It was a chance to get out of my comfort zone. As for the money-making element, I netted fifty-eight dollars after training expenses my first season. If I could find that teenager I had sat next to in class, I would just give it to him.

"Learn, learn, learn" is another key principle of LITSG. Curiosity is a foundation of learning. Every day is an opportunity to learn something new. Embrace this opportunity and make sure you finish every day knowing more than when you started it. Learn something new or develop something you already know. You only have a finite number of minutes to "spend" today. Make sure some are spent learning.

WHY, WHY, WHY

I start with the premise of always asking why. Youth learn at such a rapid pace in part because of their curiosity. Why, why, why? This is the most commonly used word in the vocabulary of a six-year-old. And if you have had this "conversation" with a six-year-old, you will know "because" is not a sufficient answer. "Because" is usually followed by another why? In the technologically advanced society we live in today, the internet and Google make information fast, efficient, and nearly free. However, too often we don't proactively seek to learn and grow. And when we do inquire, we usually spend time asking the wrong questions like where or when or who. But *why* is the more intriguing question.

Let me give you some examples. *Why* do we do things the way we do? *Why* have we done it this way in the past? Or maybe, *why* haven't we done it this way in the past? *Why* do we make certain assumptions? *Why* not consider thinking differently?

Why is powerful to the LITSG philosophy because it drives learning. As I focus on maximizing each minute, I often ask why to ensure the task at hand is a good use of time. Why opens doors to new opportunities. Why leads to new insights and curiosity. Curiosity leads to reframing and rethinking. Reframing and rethinking help me find happiness and value in each minute.

I constantly strive to learn. With a finite number of minutes available and an infinite amount of knowledge to garner, every day is a chance to learn something new.

Happiness requires continued personal growth and new challenges. It helps to avoid stagnation. We have formal learning opportunities like college, graduate and professional school, and continuing education. More importantly, we have so many informal opportunities and platforms for learning. In the current world, technology makes many of these informal opportunities accessible, efficient, and inexpensive.

Books, blogs, and articles exist on every imaginable topic. Podcasts, TED Talks, and YouTube videos present other formats for acquiring knowledge. For me, it is merely a desire to learn as much as possible, and thus it is all of the above formats, at various times.

More than any other format or opportunity, I find podcasts and audio books the most efficient manner for gathering information, in part because of the ability to multitask. Let's be careful not to overplay multitasking. Ample evidence suggests that attempting to do multiple things simultaneously often impedes your ability to do any one task well.

No doubt, acquiring knowledge requires concentration. But the ability to receive information in an audio format while on daily jogs, or while driving, is one way to make use of every minute wisely. Those minutes are otherwise "empty" minutes. They serve a primary purpose like exercise or getting from one place to another. But the ability to fill those minutes with learning, without in any way competing with or hampering the primary purpose, is the beauty of learning through audio.

Be constantly curious. Challenge assumptions. Be deliberate and thoughtful in setting and accomplishing learning goals. Most importantly, seek to learn and have an open mind about your ability to learn constantly. Your learning mindset is crucial to your success in acquiring new knowledge and skills.

MINDSET AND LEARNING

In her book *Mindset: The New Psychology of Success* (2016), Stanford professor of psychology Carol Dweck argues the world is made up of people with two primary mindsets. A growth mindset is one of control and the belief that intelligence and other personality traits can be learned and developed over time. A fixed mindset is one that lacks control and the belief that intelligence and other personality traits are static and can't be changed over time.

A fixed mindset leads to behaviors that are generally confirmatory of our innate skills and traits. This mindset avoids challenges and obstacles. A person with this mindset does not believe effort matters. Further, the fixed mindset ignores or questions feedback and criticism. Those who have a fixed mindset believe they are naturally gifted in some way, and that effort serves no role. They fear failure and will strive to prove how gifted they are. Learning and effort are not attributes of who they are.

Your fundamental approach to life and your learning mindset leads to actions and behaviors consistent with this underlying belief. A growth mindset is fundamental to success and happiness. It is core to the LITSG philosophy of always trying to learn and improve. Those who believe they can learn, change, and adapt have a greater sense of agency and control of their lives. A growth mindset embraces challenges and works to overcome obstacles. The growth mindset strongly ties effort to success and seeks feedback for improvement and learning. A growth mindset opens you up to continuous learning and improvement. Failure is just another step along the road to success.

Those with a growth mindset believe we always have an opportunity to learn, either now or at some point in the future. They may not be able to complete the task right now, but with work and learning, they can complete it in the future. This is referred to by Dweck as "not yet." It is a brilliant explanation of what it takes to be constantly learning. If I believe I can learn and improve no matter what, the opportunity is there every day. And even if a specific skill or knowledge is not there for me yet, the very use of the term "yet" demonstrates an opportunity in the future. And that future may very well be later today.

As part of my LITSG philosophy, I have an extreme growth mindset. Given a finite number of minutes in life, I dedicate substantial time to learning and growing. We have so much to learn and so many opportunities to gain skills and knowledge. Learning comes from everywhere, but I am deliberate about learning.

My learning today often comes from reading news sources and staying abreast of current events. My learning also comes from classes and webinars. During COVID, many organizations made unique and interesting learning experiences available in an online webinar format. This made learning much more efficient, and it appears to have stuck in a post-COVID world.

Books are also an amazing source of ideas and knowledge. My extreme growth mindset pushes the boundaries on what I currently know and what I can learn. As a core precept, I believe I know very little in the spectrum of the world's available knowledge, and thus there are vast opportunities to grow and learn every day.

ARE YOU KIDDING... WRITE A BOOK?

I always wanted to write a book. It was a concept, an idea, a dream. It was theoretical, but I never did anything with it until COVID shut the world down and I had a chance to hop off the treadmill of life and think about new challenges and opportunities to learn. At the encouragement of my wife, I sat down and put pen to paper and *The Life Is Too Short Guy: Strategies to Make Every Day the Best Day Ever* was born.

The experience was a marathon, up and down hills, around bends, and through tunnels. As a marathon runner, I often felt like this book journey was similar to a marathon journey. First, I didn't know where to start. How do you "train" to write? So, I hopped on the internet and searched and searched. I found my way to an amazing program, which provided me with the "training plan."

I was amped up with adrenaline and couldn't wait to get off the starting line. I wrote fast and furiously. Then I questioned my "training." I became fatigued at times. Was I doing it correctly? Where was I going? How would I get there? I needed to learn more. Hills and turns and long "training" sessions were all part of the journey that got me to the book-writing finish line. And as with my marathon training, I believed I could, and I invested time and energy in finding the right resources to learn and succeed.

So much was new. From the writing to the editing, to the cover design, I was learning each day. And beyond the book, I learned how to build a website, set up new social media accounts, and develop and execute a marketing strategy. Not once did I question if I could learn how to do it. No doubt, at times it felt overwhelming, but that is part of the beauty of the growth mindset. I just kept plugging away and researching and talking to people to acquire knowledge and skills.

As you read this book, reflect on the fact that an extreme growth mindset helped me learn and accomplish this dream. Now, think about your dream. Believing you can learn what you need to accomplish this dream is your growth mindset. Go learn today. Don't waste another precious minute.

LITSG REFLECTIONS

1. How would you characterize your primary mindset? Growth or fixed? Are there times when you are more growth or more fixed?

2. Failure provides a unique and compelling learning and growth opportunity. What recent failure were you able to learn from?

3. What three things have you always wanted to learn or get better at, but you haven't made the effort?

4. Of those three things, which one is most interesting and compelling to you? What do you have to do today to start on a path to learn or improve on that one key area of growth?

CHAPTER 8:

TAKE A CHANCE AND GET IT DONE TODAY

Take a chance! All life is a chance. The man who goes farthest is generally the one who is willing to do and dare.

—DALE CARNEGIE

Get uncomfortable! It's okay. We all find a comfort zone in life, a place of happiness and contentment. I found mine and enjoy hanging out there at times. Human nature boxes us into this zone, and LITSG pushes us out of it—actually, shoves us out of it. It's time to get out of your comfort zone today. For me, writing this book pushed me way outside my comfort zone. Sure, I like writing, but a book? On my author journey, I was constantly uncomfortable as I had so much to learn about writing, positioning, marketing, editing, etc.

As we continue our LITSG journey, another key principle is to "take a chance and get it done today." As a practical matter, it is easier to make excuses for why not, rather than justifications for why. My greatest accomplishments and happiness have come from taking chances and pushing myself to get it done... *today.*

TAKING CHANCES CHANGED MY LIFE

In high school, it was pretty easy for me to coast along academically. I ticked off As without much effort until I took chemistry my junior year. For the first time, I was staring at a B, maybe even a C+. Not possible. Couldn't happen. Chemistry was about to blemish my nearly perfect academic record. It felt like the world was coming to an end. Wow, I clearly lacked perspective at sixteen years old.

As the December holidays approached, I spoke to my guidance counselor about my irrational fear of not getting an A. He suggested I consider switching from an honors level course to a traditional chemistry class. My initial reaction was a vehement no. I would work harder. I wouldn't let honors-level chemistry beat me. I spent an inordinate amount of time and energy thinking about it over the holiday break and decided I would take a chance and switch to a regular chemistry class. It felt like one of the biggest decisions of my life. I realize it is incredibly insignificant looking back, but as a sixteen-year-old who had few problems in the world, it was a big deal. This was one of the first big "risks" I was taking.

You are probably asking how I could consider switching to an "easier" class as taking a chance. Taking a chance doesn't always mean doing something harder. Sometimes it means realizing a better path to your goals exists.

Sometimes it is realizing you are in the wrong place or situation. Sometimes it is about changing the setting. Often, taking a chance and getting out of your comfort zone equals pushing yourself harder, but in this case, it was about finding the right place for me.

As we returned from break in January of 1990, I visited my guidance counselor and told him I wanted to take the chance and switch classes. I showed up the first day of the third quarter in my new chemistry class. The teacher greeted me and looked around the room to see where he would sit me. A cute girl in the middle of the class smiled and said there was a seat behind her. I sat there, and she started flirting with me. As I put my feet up on the back of her chair, she started to untie my shoes each day during class. Then she would pass notes back to me.

I started dating that cute girl a few months later. Now, thirty-two years later, I am happily married to her. I concede I am not as strong of a chemist as I might have been had I slogged through chemistry honors, but it all worked out for the best. Had I never taken the chance to try a new chemistry class, I am not sure if I would have ever met my wife. That was a chance that truly changed my life.

Professionally, the big chance I took in life was leaving the "comfortable" confines of Wall Street for a small entrepreneurial endeavor. Days after graduating from law school in 2000, I joined Citigroup in its investment banking division and remained there for nine years. In 2009, I walked out on a Friday and started a new role at Brookfield Asset Management the following Monday.

Both were challenging roles, with all the trappings of big corporate life. Both offered great positions and all the resources I could possibly need. I had great teams and really enjoyed what I was doing. Both were comfortable, and I took a real risk in leaving such great opportunities.

Early in my career at Citi, I met an analyst. This analyst spent a few years on Wall Street before returning home to the Midwest to launch a senior housing business. First, he acquired nursing homes and then developed them. For years we kept in touch, and for years he encouraged me to join him to help build his development company. Finally, in 2013 I took what truly felt like the biggest risk of my life and walked out of a very comfortable role at an exceptional company, Brookfield, and became employee number sixteen at the development company. My role and that company have evolved and transformed over the last decade, and today I am the CEO and Chairman of a public company called Invesque. But without being willing to take a chance and leave Brookfield, I would not be running a public company today.

EXCUSES SUCK! STOP WITH EXCUSES

For years I considered the opportunity at that development company. For years I said things like, "My background is more suitable for Wall Street than a start-up," or "They won't survive because...," or "If I leave Brookfield, I will really disappoint my team." It is so easy to make excuses. I can't because... I probably shouldn't because... I would, but...

If you are going to take a chance and get it done today, the first thing you need to do is stop making excuses. I know this is hard as we generally like to stay in our comfort zone. This requires real work and commitment.

I have had so many opportunities in my life to use an excuse to avoid doing something. However, I go out of my way to defeat excuses. I look at excuses as personal challenges. I proactively say, "I know this happened, but I won't let it stop me." I take what could be an excuse and use it as a motivator.

I am an avid runner. Sometimes, injuries or illness require me to slow down or stop. But I avoid this excuse at all costs. A few days after completing a marathon, I am out training again. Sometimes I take a day or two off, but not longer than that.

Just recently I stepped to the starting line in a 5K race and didn't feel well. I got to the first mile and vomited, which is highly unusual for me. I have run dozens of races, and I have never vomited on a course (although, I certainly have after a race). Regardless, this was a chance for me to say, "Not my day," and walk off. But I wouldn't allow that thought to get in my head. I paused to puke and got right back out on the course and finished the race in a reasonable time. The "puke break" was so short and smooth, it almost appeared to be part of the racing strategy.

Later, I learned I had COVID. Feeling a bit worn out and exhibiting minor symptoms, I still went out at 6 a.m. each morning the week after the race to train. Given that I wasn't with anyone and I was outdoors, I wasn't exposing anyone. The point is that I didn't use it as an excuse. In fact, I went out of my way to say, "COVID won't slow me down."

I had other major milestones in my life when I could have used an excuse. October 21, 2017, was one of the most challenging days of my life. I arrived at a tailgate before a home Rutgers football game when my brother called to tell me that our mother had passed away. I was close with my mom and had watched her health deteriorate for a decade after my father passed away. She had lived in a nursing home for the last year, and I knew she didn't have much time left. Regardless, this call hit me hard. I was shocked and grief stricken. I told him to give me a few minutes to take it in, and I would call him back. I leaned over and put my hands on my knees and cried right there at the entrance to the Rutgers president's house, where we were going for the tailgate. My stomach muscles contracted, and I felt sick. Life changed for me forever. Now both my parents were gone, and I felt empty and lonely.

I was devastated, but I would not use this as an excuse. I was going to rally to make this day as good as I possibly could. I realize this may sound strange, but this is an extreme example of avoiding excuses. After calling the funeral home and my close friend Adlai, Jenn and I took the girls to the tailgate and then we went to the Rutgers football game. After the game, we spent time notifying friends and family and planning the funeral. Then we went to a cousin's bat mitzvah that evening.

Most people would see the death of a loved one as an excuse to cancel plans. LITSG is not most people. I used it as a motivator. No excuses. I knew Mom had passed, but I wouldn't let it stop me. Even more importantly, I knew Mom would have wanted me to go on with my day and my life. To a certain degree, staying caught up in the activity of the day helped me cope and avoid reality. It wasn't easy. I struggled to make it through each step that day, but I didn't want to make an excuse. Stop making excuses.

REFRAMING FEAR AND RISK

Now that the excuses are behind us, let's talk about taking chances. The biggest reasons we don't take chances are two horrible words: *fear* and *risk*. They reek of negativity and make me want to stop as I read them. As you think of the word fear, the associations you probably have are dread, terror, anxiety, fright, worry, etc. As you think about the word risk, the associations you probably have are failure, danger, peril, hazard, etc. But this is the problem. We collectively associate the wrong words and images with these concepts, and this prevents us from taking chances.

What if we reframed fear as Focus Entirely on Alternative Responses. As you think about fear and what it could mean, think about it as an opportunity. Think about an alternative response to the situation. Wow, I really don't have anything meaningful to fear. The fear is irrational and excessive. Even if that happens, it isn't that bad. Fear is relative and I need to find a way to realize it is insignificant here.

What if we reframed risk as Resist Instinct and Start with Knowledge. Look at the risk factors and don't focus on the negative, but rather start with real knowledge. How bad can it be? What is the worst that can happen? How can I mitigate those risks? The problem with RISK is it is often instinctual rather than knowledge based. Pause, rationally look at the risk, and reframe it as such.

Facing a life-threatening injury, former college football player Eric LeGrand learned to reframe both risk and fear. He lost mobility but gained a new perspective on life through his AHA! moment. And his major AHA! moment not only impacted him but inspired him to motivate others. As his initials indicate, Eric Legrand bELieves.

WHEN A FORMER ELITE ATHLETE BELIEVES
As ardent Rutgers football fans, my family and I attend almost every home game and even some away games. Rutgers athletics has always been a big passion for us. Jenn and I took Amanda and Jess to see Rutgers play Army at MetLife Stadium on October 16, 2010. It was one of many games we had been to and one of many we would go to in the future. But for Eric LeGrand, this would be the day that changed his life forever.

Eric was a local New Jersey kid who grew up just a few miles from Rutgers. By 2010, he was having a successful junior year on the field as a defensive tackle and special teams player. In the fourth quarter of the game that day, Eric joined his teammates on special teams to defend the kick return. Knowing his job was to stop the runner with the ball, he barreled down the field at full speed and crashed the crown of his head into the shoulder of the ball carrier.

My family and I held our breath and stared silently as Eric lay on the field motionless. We had seen many football-related injuries before, but this one had a more serious and eerie feeling to it. His time down on the ground became longer as numerous trainers, coaches, and other officials went over to help. A motorized cart rolled out, and Eric was placed on a backboard and taken to the exit tunnel on the cart. As he rode through the tunnel, his new life journey had just begun.

News trickled out shortly after the game and in the ensuing days. We learned that Eric broke two cervical vertebrae and was given a grim prognosis. "Once they did the CAT scan, they pulled my mom into a room and said, 'Your son has fractured his C3 and C4 vertebrae and he will be paralyzed from the neck down for the rest of his life. He will never walk again and never breathe on his own and never eat solid foods. We're hoping he is strong enough to make it through surgery,'" Eric told me during my interview with him.

Eric spent two weeks in the hospital before transferring to long-term rehab. He was determined to walk again and breathe on his own. On Thanksgiving Day 2010, he was briefly removed from the ventilator. He said, "It's not even whether you keep breathing; it's whether you keep breathing how you want to breathe." By January 2011, he was breathing on his own.

Eric's AHA! moment came just a few days after the catastrophic injury when he was lying in the hospital bed overwhelmed by the show of support. "They were having a prayer service for me at the College Avenue gym. I remember getting all the pictures and whatnot from that day. I was seeing banners hanging out the fraternity windows. That moment was like *wow*, this is really something special and bigger than I ever thought." Eric realized he had a responsibility now to inspire and motivate others. He was always a positive "happy-go-lucky person" but now realized he could use his situation to inspire others to accomplish their dreams. This became his life purpose.

"I'm responsible to show that with my situation, and everything that I am so limited in doing, I can I still go out and defy the odds. So why can't you? I can't lift up my head. I can't move. I can't drive myself. I can't feed myself, yet I run a foundation, I have my own business. I am still in the public doing my sports broadcasting. I'm doing all these things with only the ability to move my shoulders and above. Why would you limit yourself and your potential and everything you can do?"

The journey for Eric is a challenging one, with numerous ups and downs. In a special moment just over a year after his injury, he rejoined his teammates for a home game against West Virginia. A freakishly early snowstorm blanketed the field as Jenn, my father-in-law Steve, and I sat in the stands chilled to the bone. Eric rolled out in his electric wheelchair holding the team's symbolic axe and flanked by teammates on both sides. It was a heartwarming, tear-inducing moment as fans stood and cheered. That image appeared on the cover of *Sports Illustrated* and was voted the Fans' Choice Best Moment of 2011.

In addition to realizing his purpose in life is to motivate and inspire others to take chances and live a full life, Eric also learned to be more patient and overlook small setbacks. Before his injury, if something small went wrong, it would drive him crazy, and he would get frustrated. Now, he accepts that things take him longer and that sometimes things don't go as planned. "That is just part of life."

And the biggest realization in Eric's life as a result of his AHA! moment? "No matter what we're going through, no matter what it is, no matter what cards we are dealt, it can always be worse. Even when you get a card that says you might die in three months, it always could be worse. You could have one day to live. If you look at it like that, look at it from a perspective like that, there will be a lot of joyful moments throughout your journey."

Eric reframed fear and risk and put all the excuses aside. He returned to Rutgers and gave the commencement speech in 2014. He even realized his dream of being a professional football player when he was symbolically signed to an NFL contract by his former head coach Greg Schiano who was then coaching the Tampa Bay Buccaneers. Eric also won the Jimmy V Award for Perseverance at the ESPYs. The list of accolades goes on and on. He started a foundation focused on spinal cord research and became a sports analyst for ESPN, Sirius XM, the Big Ten Network, and Rutgers radio. He is also an entrepreneur who launched his own line of clothing and his own brand of coffee.

Eric learned to take chances and not make excuses despite all the challenges he faces. He is the quintessential model of LITSG as he makes the most of life. He takes chances and gets things done. He has no regrets.

TOP FIVE REGRETS OF THE DYING

Most people really start to focus on regrets at the end of their lives. The word "regrets" has a negative connotation. I prefer to look at setbacks or past experiences as opportunities to learn and do things differently. Australian palliative care nurse Bronnie Ware wrote a book called *The Top 5 Regrets of the Dying* (2011) based on her experiences with patients who had less than three months to live. "My patients were those who had gone home to die. Some incredibly special times were shared. I was with them for the last three to twelve weeks of their lives."

So what were the top five regrets of those dying?

1. I wish I'd had the courage to live a life true to myself, not the life others expected of me.
2. I wish I hadn't worked so hard.
3. I wish I'd had the courage to express my feelings.
4. I wish I had stayed in touch with my friends.
5. I wish I had let myself be happier.

Based on these regrets, Bronnie was able to cull some important lessons. Rather than wait until we are in our final days of life, today is the day to reflect on these regrets and think about what they mean. No one refers to "not having enough money" or "not working hard enough." Those are not priorities of the dying who learned it was best to never prioritize money or work over things that truly matter.

Many looked back and realized they lived a life with dreams unfulfilled. Most people had not honored at least half of their dreams. Dreaming is only the first step. Failing to move the dream forward is a missed opportunity and one that many regret. Failing to take a chance seems like one of the biggest regrets most have as they approach death.

Rachel Wallins set out to change her life to a Life of Yes after battling cancer. Rather than think about excuses or why not, her AHA! moment was to just say yes, yes, yes!

THE LIFE OF YES

"The one thing I decided to start in 2020, the year after my surgery, was to make it the Year of Yes. I decided I was going to say yes to everything. And then 2021 became the Year of Yes. And then 2022 became the Year of Yes. And I just realized I was living a Life of Yes," Rachel told me during our interview.

For her fiftieth birthday in 2019, Rachel was ready to celebrate in a big way. She and her husband Jeff rented a yacht and invited fifty of her closest friends from around the country to join them for the celebration of a lifetime. "It was an awesome night, and I felt so surrounded by love. It was the best day of my life."

Five days later, Rachel had a massive seizure at work. She was talking to someone and forgot who she was talking to, why she was talking to them, and even the name of the company she worked for. She drove herself to urgent care where she couldn't answer basic questions like what medications she was taking or when her birthday was. She was admitted to the emergency room of the local hospital and later that evening the doctor told her she had suffered a stroke.

After a week in the hospital and numerous tests, an MRI revealed a two-centimeter tumor in her brain. Three weeks later she was at Memorial Sloan Kettering Hospital in New York City to have the tumor removed.

One month later, she returned to work where she had been recently promoted to the role of chief human resource officer. "This is where I think the AHA! moment comes." She struggled when she returned to the role of CHRO. "So, it started to dawn on me that I had changed. And that I couldn't go back to who I had been because who I was, was dead. And at the moment I found out that I had a tumor, I ceased to exist. And a new person started to come in and that new person was a person for whom all of the previous constructs were completely broken. Because my own mortality felt more present. So when you do that, and when you feel that way, you look at the world very differently."

Rachel realized that her old sense of success and goal setting had changed. Before her diagnosis, she would continue to set high bars, and every time she reached a goal, she would raise the bar rather than enjoy the success. Goal chasing was her life. She was done chasing the goals in an effort to find happiness. She quit her job and started her own company as an executive coach and leadership and team development professional.

Rachel believes her biggest AHA! epiphany was the change in her perspective on risk and fear. "Because in my head, I was like, *What's the worst that can happen?* It's already happened to me personally. Everything else is just bullshit. It doesn't get much worse than being told you have brain cancer. So I decided that I would start my own business and I would do what I needed to do and work hard. And if it didn't work out, it didn't work out, but I didn't really care."

Rachel started to think about risk and fear differently in her personal life as well. "I decided that I was going to say yes to everything. So, we went parasailing, which I've been petrified of because I hate heights. Yes. I decided to try skiing. I don't like the cold. I don't like going fast. But I said yes. When my son Nicky would say, 'Do you want to play basketball?' Yes. When my daughter Charlotte would say, 'Do you want to play rummy cube?' Yes. When my husband would say, 'Let's go try X, Y, and Z,' I would say yes."

Rachel wants to encourage others to live in the moment, overcome fears, and take risks. In doing so, she exemplifies the LITSG life. "But it's stupid to not live a Year of Yes. Or a Life of Yes. Because everybody has an expiration date, and you don't know what your expiration date is. Some people are like, 'Oh, I'm just working 'til I can retire.' Why are we waiting? I'd rather spend the money now. So I now own my own business. I'm having the Year of Yes. I'm making time to see my friends. I go to the gym five days a week because I love it. I'm taking up tennis. I took myself on a date for the first time maybe ever last week. And for people who are not reinventing themselves like that, I feel sorry for them because they're not. They're not getting it."

A Life of Yes also requires us to say no sometimes, based on a deliberate assessment of how to use finite minutes. The reality is we only have so many minutes, so we can't possibly say yes to everything. Each person must decide what to say yes to and what to say no to based on how to maximize the value of each minute. Saying no to things that don't bring us happiness and joy opens those minutes to saying yes to things we might have otherwise passed on.

LITSG requires taking chances and getting it done today. I emphasize the today element in part because it adds urgency to the goal. It is hard to take a chance, and the first step is wanting to take the chance. The next key step is actually doing it, and delay and procrastination are enemies of getting it done. Take a chance and get it done today!

1. Taking a chance means being proactive. First, it means identifying the chances you want to take. What are five chances you want to take right now?

2. Stop the excuses. They are easy to hide behind but harmful. What excuses have you recently made to avoid taking a chance? What excuse are you not going to let get in your way moving forward?

3. Risk and fear are negative words. Reframe them in a positive way. Eliminating risk and fear is a significant step in taking a chance. How can you think about risk and fear differently?

4. Leadership guru and bestselling author John Maxwell asked, "When was the last time you did something for the first time?" Well?

CHAPTER 9:

CAN'T MAKE IT ALONE

Being human, we are imperfect. That's why we need each other. To catch each other when we falter. To encourage each other when we lose heart. Some may lead; others may follow. But none of us can go it alone.

—HILLARY CLINTON

Humans need one another. Social interactions, friends, family, and community are all vital elements of LITSG. Whether you are an introvert or an extrovert, it doesn't matter. Social interaction is one of the key drivers of happiness. In my finite minutes, I am constantly looking for new interactions, friends, acquaintances, relationships, and buddies. It is not about accumulating a certain number of friends. It is about building communities, having a sense of belonging, sharing good memories, and writing your story with others.

Gradations exist along the friendship continuum, as do differences between true friends and broad acquaintances. You can approach some with a friendly disposition. True friends are special but rare. They are, however, the most valuable. Having a handful of friends you can count on no matter what is vital to your success and happiness.

I think about it as a "friendship galaxy" with me at the center. It is rare I am the center of any galaxy, but as it relates to relationships, we are each the center of our own galaxy. It starts with my innermost friendship ring and my wife Jenn. I have no closer friend and no one I can rely on more. We have been together our entire adult lives, and even some of our teenage years. I don't really know life without her.

The next ring is my immediate family. In addition to my daughters, my in-laws Doris and Steve are in this ring as I have grown very close to them, knowing them for over two-thirds of my life. I am truly fortunate to have met them so young and grown and matured with them as parents. These two family-oriented rings combined, give me the foundation to grow and build a broader social network. Moving outward, I have a handful of close personal friends in the next inner circle, which is the next ring. After this, I am reaching out into the galaxy. The rings get bigger and fuzzier. The next circle is a much larger group of acquaintances. These are people I know reasonably well and keep in touch with regularly. The next ring is further out in the galaxy, and the stars here are a bit dimmer and deeper in the universe. But there might be a close friend out there waiting to be discovered.

EVERYONE CAN BE A FRIEND

We crave social interaction. If there is one thing learned from the forced social experiment we call COVID, we collectively missed so much of what we take for granted. Those daily interactions with friends, colleagues, and strangers completely shut down during the forced isolation that COVID required. The smallest human interactions disappeared, and we can learn so much from this. We missed dinners and celebrations with close friends and family. We missed sporting events, shows, and movies with friends and even strangers. We missed casual dialogue at the local coffee shop. Until we lost it, we didn't appreciate how important it was.

Positive social interactions lead to greater happiness and fulfillment. And it doesn't require much, but it does require a deliberate daily goal of building relationships. Again, core to LITSG, we *can't make it alone*. So make an effort today to meet someone new, grow an existing relationship, or both.

Four or five mornings per week, I go out and run early. Every time I run, I pass people on the street, and I always acknowledge them. To the crossing guard I passed this morning, I said, "Good morning. Thanks so much. Stay warm. Have a great day." It took fewer than ten seconds, but it created an ongoing relationship. Not a lifelong friendship but a human relationship. That guard sees me run by a few times a week and enjoys the short positive conversation. He smiles to acknowledge the approaching runner. When I don't run for a few days, he sometimes will ask where I have been.

Minutes after my interaction with the crossing guard, I saw a dog walker and said, "Good morning. Cold day today. Stay warm." The dog walker responded, "Sure is. Stay safe." I never stop running during the brief exchange of pleasantries. But I feel a sense of connection and happiness in these interactions, and I can tell the recipient does too. I wave and smile at others I pass during my morning runs.

This approach helps me build relationships with everyone. Everyone is important in my life. The gardener, mail carrier, receptionist, and cashier all crave and enjoy positive interaction. Every opportunity I get, I engage with them. A smile, an observation, a positive comment. Maybe a question. People love answering questions, particularly about themselves. Everyone has value. Everyone appreciates being recognized. Everyone presents an opportunity to become a friend, acquaintance, or just a passing short-term relationship.

BEING A FRIENDSHIP LEADER

Strangers are merely future friends. Again, I use the term "friends" loosely. I am not talking about best friends; I am talking about an approach where everyone can be friendly and grow their social circles. As part of my LITSG philosophy, I am quick to bring people together. I look for opportunities to host social events and to introduce "strangers."

I surround myself with friends and family. Life is more fun when enjoyed with others. I often say, "It's all about the story." I like to write chapters of my story with other characters. I organize the annual buddies golf trips. A dozen of us have been going to a different golf destination for twenty-one years. I am the organizer of the high school reunions, the barbecues, and many other social gatherings.

Someone mentions, "We should plan a trip to Napa or Nashville," and I jump on it and take the lead that day. Every opportunity I get to both broaden and deepen my social networks is important to me and my happiness. A meal, a random holiday like Cinco de Mayo or Oktoberfest, or a sporting event like Rutgers Football Opening Day (deliberately in caps to emphasize the importance to me) all lend themselves to celebrations with others, and Jenn and I always find ways to celebrate. This ties nicely to the LITSG philosophy about celebrations. It doesn't have to be extravagant or over the top. The real goal is building community and collective happiness.

As I think about how best to use my finite minutes, sharing those minutes building relationships and having fun is at the top of my list. You can't make it alone. And even if you think you can, why would you want to? Life is better when shared with others.

LITSG looks to each of us to become *friendship leaders*. Every group has someone who brings the group together and is always organizing the next thing. Well, why don't you become the friendship leader? Every group can have more than one and new friendship leaders bring new perspectives and ideas. Today is your day to become a friendship leader. Text a group of friends today and organize something. Drinks? Dinner? Sporting event? What do you want to do and how can you bring others together to share in this happiness?

Ample empirical evidence demonstrates how important social interactions and community are to your long-term health and happiness. One of the most prolific studies to demonstrate this started at an Ivy League school in Boston over eighty years ago.

RELATIONSHIPS MATTER THE MOST

What makes a good life? In 1938, a Harvard physician began what would become one of the longest running studies to answer this question. The original study identified 268 men who were sophomores at Harvard between 1939 and 1944. Each of the men participated in a range of interviews, questionnaires, physicals, and psychological measurements. A second group of 456 disadvantaged, Boston area inner-city youths were later added to the study.

The study continues to this day with over eighty years of ongoing assessment and data. Some participants turned out to be "successful" while others did not. Four of the participants ran for the United States Senate, one became President of the United States, and another a best-selling author. Some died young and lonely. Some developed alcoholism and addictions. Some grappled with mental illness.

Perspectives on success changed over the course of the participants' lives. However, the one key finding about how to live a good life is *relationships matter more than anything else.* "The surprising thing is that our relationships and how happy we are in our relationships has a powerful influence on our health," Robert Waldinger, study director, a psychiatrist at Massachusetts General Hospital, and a professor at Harvard Medical School, told *The Harvard Gazette* (Mineo 2017). "Taking care of your body is important but tending to your relationships is a form of self-care, too. That, I think, is the revelation."

Good relationships keep us happier and healthier as we age. Social connections are incredibly important for happiness, health, and longevity. By contrast, those who are more socially isolated and lonely are less happy, less healthy, and live shorter lives. The correlation between happiness and health on the one hand and social relationships on the other is primarily driven by quality of relationships, not number of relationships. The power of relationships is driven by deeper, meaningful connections.

At age fifty, how satisfied participants were in their relationships was the key indicator of health at age eighty. I found this stat particularly compelling, especially as I approach my half-century mark. What was also interesting is that good relationships don't just protect the body but also the mind. Those in the closest, more trusting relationships, where each participant can count on the other to be there, had the best memory later in life. It is worth noting that relationships don't have to last a lifetime. Relationships include friends, family, and community. These groups evolve over a lifetime. For example, those happiest in retirement worked proactively to replace workmates with playmates.

Other global studies support this same conclusion. Dan Buettner is a *National Geographic* fellow and author who studies people who live in "Blue Zones." Blue Zones are the places in the world where people live the longest and are healthiest. Through his work, Buettner identified the habits of people who live far longer than the average. According to a *New York Times* article (Leland 2022), Buettner concluded, "Friends can exert a measurable and ongoing influence on your health behaviors in a way that a diet never can."

In Okinawa, Japan, women have a life expectancy of ninety, the oldest in the world. He noted that in Okinawa, people form social networks called moai, a group of friends who offer social, logistical, emotional, and even financial support for a lifetime. Buettner worked with former United States surgeon general Vivek Murthy to bring this concept of moais to cities around the US in an effort to spread the power of this social network.

We each have the opportunity to proactively seek and develop social networks. Failure to do so leads to loneliness. Even prior to the COVID pandemic, Dr. Murthy believed the US faced a massive healthcare crisis he called an "epidemic of loneliness." Murthy blamed our accelerated pace of life and the prolific spread of technology as "edging out" real relationships. He referred to this as a public health crisis of a magnitude similar to the opioid epidemic or obesity. One in five Americans said they always or often felt lonely or socially isolated, according to a 2018 study by the Kaiser Family Foundation. Today is the day to end this loneliness epidemic.

We each have the ability to be deliberate and proactive in our goal of building a strong and broader social network. Doing so not only prevents loneliness for us, but for all those we take the time to reach out to and build relationships with.

Too often, we sacrifice friendships or family relationships for other things. Unfortunately, work and material possessions are high on the priority list for many, at the expense of family and friends. LITSG presses each of us to reprioritize and realize the physical, psychological, and overall health benefits of being a part of a strong social community and network. We each define success differently. Think carefully about what success means to you.

FINAL REFLECTIONS ON "SUCCESS"

I reached the pinnacle of success in the business world. In others' eyes, my life is the epitome of success. However, aside from work, I have little joy. In the end, my wealth is only a fact of life that I am accustomed to. At this moment, lying on my bed and recalling my life, I realize that all the recognition and wealth that I took so much pride in have paled and become meaningless in the face of my death.

You can employ someone to drive the car for you, make money for you, but you cannot have someone bear your sickness for you. Material things lost can be found or replaced. But there is one thing that can never be found when it's lost—life. Whichever stage in life you're in right now, with time, you will face the day when the curtain falls.

Treasure love for your family, love for your spouse, love for your friends. Treat yourself well and cherish others. As we grow older, and hopefully wiser, we realize that a three-thousand-dollar or a thirty-dollar watch both tell the same time. You will realize that your true inner happiness does not come from the material things of this world. Whether you fly first class or economy, if the plane goes down—you go down with it.

Therefore, I hope you realize, when you have mates, buddies and old friends, brothers and sisters, who you chat with, laugh with, talk with, sing with, talk about north-south-east-west or heaven and earth, that is true happiness. Don't educate your children to be rich. Educate them to be happy. So when they grow up they will know the value of things and not the price. Eat your food as your medicine, otherwise, you have to eat medicine as your food.

The one who loves you will never leave you for another because, even if there are 100 reasons to give up, he or she will find a reason to hold on. There is a big difference between a human being and being human. Only a few really understand it. You are loved when you are born. You will be loved when you die. In between, you have to manage.

The six best doctors in the world are sunlight, rest, exercise, diet, self-confidence, and friends. Maintain them in all stages and enjoy a healthy life.

This is thought to be the essay Steve Jobs wrote in his last days before death. You can find it easily all over the internet. There remains debate about whether in fact he did write it. The authenticity is irrelevant as the message is thought-provoking and meaningful. The belief that he wrote it, whether or not factually accurate, is sufficient to reflect on its meaning. Substitute any name you want for the author, and it is still meaningful. You can substitute your own name. As you read it, think about your life. Does it resonate? I hope not, but I suspect it does for many in some way.

Why wait until you realize your final minutes are ticking away to have this epiphany? Today is the day you can take immediate action and alter your path to happiness and fulfillment. Why wait another minute? It may only take a minute.

IT TAKES SO LITTLE BUT CAN MEAN SO MUCH

It's quick, easy, and can change your life in such a positive way. You know you want to stay connected, enhance relationships, or grow new relationships. What can you do today to accomplish this? You can use so many small, easy tools today and every day to grow the power of your social network.

When was the last time you randomly checked in with someone with no particular agenda? A friend, acquaintance, or family? You weren't looking for help or an answer. You just decided to shoot a quick text or email. Or even better, you just picked up the phone. Try it today. You will be amazed by the positive response you will receive.

When was the last time you handwrote a note? Yup, a good old-fashioned handwritten note? Each year around the holiday season in December, I write a handful of notes to people who matter to me. It can be a short note telling them how important they are to me and wishing them all the best. A sentence or two to reminisce. As we all get caught up in informal emails or sterile holiday cards, think about how powerful it would be to receive a thoughtful, personalized, handwritten note.

Have you sent a small, unsolicited, random gift to someone lately? I love to send someone a book, audio book, or random trinket that specifically reminds me of them. Ever receive a random gift you weren't expecting? I was recently on a trip to Nashville with a group of close friends. The trip came about when the same group was on a friends' trip to Napa, and we talked about Nashville. I booked a rental house within a few days of the conversation. It went from theoretical concept to reality in minutes.

As you might know, Nashville can be a fun town. We hung out on a rooftop bar the first day where we saw someone using colorful, novelty party straws. I made a big deal about how cool they were and how I wanted to find them. Well, about a week later, a package of those straws waited for me. Talk about making my day! My friend Carolyn saw the opportunity and sent me this small gift. I smiled and embraced the moment. Someone thought about me and took a few minutes to make my day better.

Are you ever sitting around, and an old picture pops up on a digital frame or on your social media feed? Maybe some amazing event that happened years ago? Well, I will take that picture and forward it on to someone in that picture to remind him of what a wonderful experience we had together and to evoke a special memory. What a great way to reengage in a positive way with someone you might not have seen or spoken to in years.

And finally, how about a random article from a newspaper or magazine that has meaning to a friend? I love to read newspapers. Almost every day I will see an article, and it jogs a memory of someone. It usually is about a topic we have discussed or a topic of particular interest to them. When I do, I send them the article. It shows them I am thinking about them and that I took the time to send something of interest to them.

All of these ideas are fairly small and not that time consuming. Minutes, literally minutes. None really requires a significant investment. However, doing a few of these small outreaches each day helps strengthen and grow your social network. None of us can make it alone. LITSG believes a happy and fulfilled life is best lived surrounded by people we know and love. Invite others in to help you write your life story. It's all about the story.

LITSG REFLECTIONS

1. The first step in building and growing a social network is to be proactive and deliberate. Write down three friends you haven't spoken to in a while and who you will reach out to this week.

2. We have so many easy tools to engage with new and old friends. What tools resonated the most with you? What tools do you use that aren't mentioned in this book?

3. Everyone can become a friend. Engage with a stranger today and get to know her. Learn about her and what makes her tick. Your interest makes her happier and this, in turn, makes you happier.

4. Sometimes work or other commitments get in the way of building relationships with friends and family. Be aware of this and strive to avoid it. Make today the day you prioritize building and strengthening your relationships and social network.

CHAPTER 10:

CRAZY RED HAIR AND FACE PAINT—PASSION

Nothing is as important as passion. No matter what you want to do with your life, be passionate.

—JON BON JOVI

Half red, half white, frizzy and standing straight up away from my head. This wig could have been used by a clown. Some might say it was. I put it on right after the face paint. The paint was half black and half red. I was meticulously neat about the paint application. Wig on, check! Face paint on, check! Ready for battle, I headed to the stadium to suffer through another Rutgers football loss. As a newly minted alum in the mid-1990s, I was *fired up* about a losing team.

Let me clarify what I mean by losing. I graduated in May 1995. In the subsequent decade, the team won a whopping twenty-seven games. That's twenty-seven games in *ten* seasons. To be clearer, they lost eighty-five games over the same decade.

It didn't matter. I was passionate about Rutgers football. No one would mistake me as a bandwagon fan. We didn't have a bandwagon to hop on. Yet I was there week after week hoping for a miracle. I talked about winning seasons and bowl bids. My credibility (what little I might have had) was shot after a "special" winless season in 1997. Yup, zero-eleven. But I still tailgated and showed up at games—even in November when the ground was frozen, you could see your breath, and only a few thousand people attended. And that few thousand included the teams, bands, cheerleaders, press, security, vendors, and everyone else in the vicinity of the stadium. I was passionate, and it never waned.

What are you passionate about? This is one of my favorite questions when I interview people. I have done hundreds of interviews over my career. I have interviewed people for a broad range of roles from interns to entry-level staff, managers, executives, and board members. The interviews were for different companies and in different industries. But the question is universal and applicable in all cases.

What are you passionate about?

Amazingly, it throws most people off. In about 90 percent of the interviews the first response is, "Wow, that is a good question." Then, I often get questions such as, "What do you mean? In what context? Work?" I always respond by saying, "It doesn't matter. You decide."

WHY PASSION?

Passion is a powerful word with powerful implications. It is a much stronger word than interests or hobbies. Going back to the interview question, I might have asked, "What do you do for fun?" or, "Tell me about some of your interests." But this is boring. This refers to an average life, not an exceptional LITSG life. Answering questions about interests or hobbies sets the tone for going through the motions in life, not embracing life.

But passion evokes a different response. Passion refers to a meaningful interest. An excessive level of enthusiasm, energy, and commitment. Think Rutgers football, face paint, and a hopeless team. Something you are "all in" on. Something you care about deeply. To a certain degree, it is how you define yourself. Passion helps define identity. If you can't figure out what your passion is, today is the day to start focusing on finding your passion. Or, if your interest level is waning in something you were historically passionate about, it's time to look for new passions.

LEAVE YOUR MARK

To make every day the best day ever, I seek to have an impact on the world around me. I don't want to be an observer in life who passes through merely as a visitor. Regardless of the place or situation or circumstances, I want to make sure the world knows I was there.

If you choose to participate in something, passion is the level of commitment LITSG expects. Passion is a fervent desire to be a part of something and have a positive impact on it. Impact is an important word as you think about passion.

So, what is something you are passionate about? As I noted in my interview question dialogue, you choose the passion. Maybe it is an affiliation with a religious organization, a sports team, a school, a charity, a club, or a hobby. The list is endless. You need to start by asking what excites you and how do you make it a passion? And continue to look for new passions. There is no one formula for finding passion. It is a personal process of exploring life. Don't overthink it. If it makes you happy, makes you smile, and you want to embrace it, go for it. And you don't have to commit to one passion, nor do you have to commit to the same passion forever. You can set a goal today (and add it to your Goals Grid) to take steps to grow hobbies and interests into a passion.

Passions change as life evolves. Kevin McHugh overcame a handful of major life setbacks before he found his passion and identity in religion.

GOD IS MY AHA! MOMENT
Some AHA! moments are an exact moment in time. Others build based on a series of AHA! moments leading to one specific moment—the moment when we each realize we need to change.

Kevin McHugh married his high school sweetheart. He met her in the summer of 1969 after his parents moved to a new community when he was sixteen years old. He was entering his junior year of high school when he first crossed paths with Jeannie. Then, in October, their life partnership began. "I remember this vividly. Getting into somebody's car to go home, and the windshield was foggy. She had just given me her phone number, and I wrote it in the foggy windshield so I could read it again." He called her and began a journey of happiness that would produce three children and last over thirty years.

In 1999 Jeannie was diagnosed with ovarian cancer that she battled for almost three years. Things took a turn for the worse while on vacation. "We were in Florida at a small beach hotel where we and her family had gone every year since we met in high school. It was now thirty-two years later. I did not know it, but she was dying." Jeannie got sick quickly on this trip. "Friends sent a nurse and social worker to visit when I described her condition. We arrived on Tuesday. On Thursday, the nurse told me the news that she had only days to live. I frantically got my three college-age kids to Florida from Ohio on Friday. She died Saturday morning while we were all there."

This wasn't an AHA! moment for Kevin. It was just the beginning of the next phase of his life. About a year later, he met Mary, his current wife. During the ensuing several years, Kevin believes he accumulated AHA! moments through life experiences that led him to learn to let go. Along the way, he had what he calls "a powerful AHA! within the AHA!, which I call sobriety." Kevin had been struggling with the loneliness associated with losing Jeannie and a challenging marriage to Mary.

One day after a fight, Mary got in her car and drove away. Kevin called a close friend of over twenty-five years to vent and complain, and the friend asked him if he had a drink yet. "No, but that is a damn good idea," Kevin said. His friend told him not to, but rather to go empty his liquor cabinet and then abruptly hung up. He told him to call him back when Kevin was done. "I remember vividly sitting on the floor. This open cabinet underneath the bar, and I poured and emptied probably sixty bottles of liquor. I had so many bottles because I was the guy in the neighborhood who could make 85 percent of the book—Mr. Boston's book on drinks and cocktails."

This was the ultimate AHA! moment for Kevin. "Now, for me to robotically get up and go to the liquor cabinet and do what I did, I think, is just a conclusion of something that had been in my heart for the last year. I kind of knew... most alcoholics actually do."

The next day Kevin flew to Florida for an industry conference, and that evening, he attended a fancy dinner. He explains it as "the perfect scenario" for what he should have avoided. He was in a beautiful mansion attending a dinner with about fifty other successful business executives, and the waiter came around to pour water and then followed with a bottle of expensive red wine. Kevin turned down the glass of wine once, but the waiter returned. He flipped his glass over, and the gentlemen sitting next to him asked, "Are you a friend of Bill's?" Not understanding the reference, Kevin said, "No, I am here with Jane." His table partner explained it was a reference to Bill Wilson, founder of Alcoholics Anonymous. The two proceeded to the porch of this exquisite mansion, and Kevin learned about AA. They ate outside while Kevin's new friend talked about his twenty-five years of sobriety. The next day, Kevin returned to Ohio and attended his first AA meeting.

Fourteen years later, Kevin remains sober and happily married, and he credits his close friend for encouraging him to take the first step of emptying the liquor cabinet. Always a religious man, the AHA! moments associated with the death of his first wife, struggles in his second marriage, and the ultimate acknowledgment of his alcohol addiction led him to the church in a more meaningful and passionate way. This is where he found his identity and happiness. This is where he discovered his passion, and this passion guides his life today. "God, in the Christian worldview, is the big AHA! belief for me."

ALL IN

As I think about my passions in life, I have had many and have fully committed to each. As a child I was passionate about soccer. I watched soccer, played soccer, refereed soccer, and lived a soccer life. I identified fervently with soccer. I played indoors and outdoors. Soccer was my everything.

As a teenager, I was passionate about the Boy Scouts. As I previously discussed, I was all in and flew through the Boy Scout ranks quickly. I committed to becoming an Eagle Scout and took every opportunity I could to speed my path to the pinnacle. I took on leadership roles and committed to a robust merit badge schedule each summer at camp. For a teenage boy, I was passionate, committed, and a bit crazy about climbing the ranks.

As I grew up, I was passionate about high school and got actively involved in student government, sports, clubs, and pretty much everything. I was class president and on the executive board of the student council. In fact, I was even elected student council president, but the principal wouldn't allow me to be both class president and student council president. I attended all major school events and sporting events. I organized my class and led events like homecoming, the senior variety show, and prom. I loved associating with my high school and leaving my mark there. I can confidently say most people in high school saw the impact I had while I was a student. Just prior to graduation, my class voted me the student with the "most school spirit." Five hundred and fifty classmates, and I had the "most school spirit." That's impact.

Then I was off to college, and I took the "most school spirit" to an extreme. Over twenty-five years after graduating from Rutgers, I still have football and basketball season tickets. I attend many other Rutgers sporting events including home and away men's and women's soccer, field hockey, wrestling, and lacrosse. I have been active in alumni associations and on the board of the Rutgers Foundation. I guest lecture to Rutgers Business School classes. I mentor and have hired many Rutgers students and alumni. I have a red car (the school color) and Rutgers license plates. Most friends and acquaintances associate me with Rutgers and consider me the single biggest Rutgers fan in the world. I am incredibly passionate about Rutgers, and I am all in, to say the least.

I exude passion and commit serious energy to so many different things. These are just a few of the many passions I have had over the course of my life. Other passions have included running, endurance sports, and golf. I have run fifteen marathons and completed one Ironman triathlon. I hired coaches and trained incredibly hard and qualified for the Boston Marathon three times. This is passion, not just a hobby. Today, writing this book and launching the *Life Is Too Short Guy* platform is one of my most compelling passions. As I previously noted, passions change as life evolves. However, the commitment to the passion does not change. I am always "all in" and take away so much joy, energy, happiness, and gratitude as my commitment to various passions grows and evolves.

WHY DOES IT MATTER?

Passion is a core component of LITSG for two primary reasons. First, we each have the ability to fully embrace something we love. As we strive to live every day as the best day ever, having something to believe in and embrace is vitally important. This is your opportunity to live a happier and more fulfilling life by committing to something you are passionate about. Have multiple passions. It ties to other LITSG principles like gratefulness. This passion becomes something so important to you, it is another element of life for which to be grateful. It also ties to *minutes matter* in that you have a finite number of minutes in your life, so why not allocate some to a true passion rather than just a passing or superficial interest?

The second important reason why passion is core to LITSG is because you *can't make it alone.* Passion leads to social connections. As you think about what you are passionate about, you will affiliate with interest groups, clubs, and like-minded people who share your passion. What better way to build friendships and social networks than to do so focused on something you are passionate about.

So, I now ask you a fairly obvious question: What's *your* passion?

LITSG REFLECTIONS

1. What is your greatest passion? What have you done to commit to and grow this passion?

2. As life changes, so do passions. Is there a passion that has been percolating that might be worth exploring? What is the next step to making this passion a part of your life today?

3. How has your passion helped define your identity? Is it consistent with who you want to be? Is your passion truly important to you?

4. How can you use your passions to grow your social networks and friendships? Do you have new opportunities to leverage passions to grow your social networks?

CHAPTER 11:

LIVE TODAY... DON'T WAIT FOR TOMORROW

Living in the moment means letting go of the past and not waiting for the future. It means living your life consciously, aware that each moment you breathe is a gift.

—OPRAH WINFREY

We all die. It is one of the most fundamental elements of life we can't control. That and the weather. I always wanted to figure out how to control the weather. However, knowing we will all die and putting it in perspective is an amazing life-changing tool and another key element of LITSG.

As we have discussed extensively, we each have the ability to control our perspective and approach to life. With this as a foundation, the ability to live today and let go of the past is the final important building block of LITSG. We can either choose to live in fear of death or choose to live in spite of death. The LITSG philosophy focuses on making the most of every day and acknowledging life is finite. Minutes are finite. Focusing on the end of life and working backward helps frame our perspective.

USING THE END AS A TOOL FOR TODAY

We don't know how or when we will die. But LITSG looks forward to the end as inspiration for now. Let's start with some foundational questions. How do you want to be remembered? Have you thought about this before? If you are like most, I suspect not. So, think about it now. Right now. Put this book down, close your eyes and think about how you want to be remembered. Take some time to think about what you want your gravestone to say. Write it down. Even if you choose cremation, the mere act of writing just a few words on a page to define your life brings clarity to the life you want to live right now. For me it is easy... *Life is too short; make every day the best day ever.* Maybe a bit much for a tombstone, but in small font, it works. Or maybe just a large tombstone!

Now, take it one step further. Write the key themes of your eulogy. Maybe even write your entire eulogy. You have more words to play with here. You have greater flexibility to weave together a story. What is your story and how will you want it portrayed? How do you want to be remembered by your closest family and friends? Frame your life story in a few pages. What resonates? What is important? How you want to be remembered is the key to how you need to live today to make every day the best day ever.

Okay, now let's take this one step further. Write your obituary. What were the salient moments and accomplishments in your life that you want the world to know about? How do you want to be defined and remembered? This is for the strangers, the ones you never met. As you look at the themes and key words on your tombstone, eulogy, and obituary, what is the story you leave behind? What is your legacy? Is this the life you are living today? If not, why not and how do you change it? Stop waiting for tomorrow. Live today.

Don't fear death. Use your ultimate demise as your motivator to live the life you want and start doing it today. Start by adding a goal to your Goals Grid to think about and define your legacy. As you do, make it your goal to live your best day ever, every day. Stop thinking about the past or focusing too much on the future. Live today.

MAKE IT YOUR LIFE, YOUR WAY

As you think about how you want to be remembered, focus on what is important to you, not to others. We too often worry about the story we are writing for others. How often do you spin your stories to portray an image that is not reality? Who cares what others think? Care about your story and living your life honestly and to the fullest.

Too often, we waste time thinking about what others have rather than who we are and what we want. We waste effort on envy rather than investing in happiness. Be happy for others, and don't measure your success in life relative to the success of friends and family.

As a society, we collectively admire so many people who we later discover are deeply troubled and unhappy. Abraham Lincoln was believed to be suicidal and had a fondness for sad songs and poems. Marilyn Monroe was married and divorced three times and died at age thirty-six of an apparent suicide. Frank Sinatra was rumored to have attempted suicide twice. Princess Diana attempted suicide at least twice and began self-harming shortly after her marriage. These are all societal icons many looked up to or envied, yet it appears they all struggled with finding happiness. Some, like entrepreneur Tony Hsieh, go out of their way to portray extreme happiness, while living a life of unhappiness.

DELIVERING HAPPINESS... OR SO IT SEEMED

Finding true happiness is a journey that is different for everyone. While the world sees great success and apparent happiness in how a person tells their story, for many, the internal mental struggles make reality far from the facade. LITSG provides a set of practical tools for embracing and improving happiness, sometimes in small ways. LITSG is not about merely portraying happiness.

Tony Hsieh built an entire billion-dollar-plus shoe company based on the premise of happiness. Happiness was foundational to the culture he built, and it started with the hiring process.

At Zappos, Hsieh used an interview technique where he asked candidates to rate their inherent luck on a scale of one to ten. After the self-assessment, job seekers were then asked to scan a newspaper and count photographs. The paper was completely fictitious and had specific quotes and headlines screaming to the reader that they can stop counting now, and in one case, they could even collect an extra one hundred dollars rather than continuing to count photos. The people who considered themselves inherently lucky generally stopped counting earlier, and those who were self-proclaimed unlucky generally missed the headlines and cues and got to the right number of pictures but missed the point.

At a Business Innovation Factory Collaborative Innovation Summit, Hsieh said, "In life, luck is really more about being open to opportunity beyond just how the task or situation presents itself." He spoke regularly about optimism and tied it in part to his business success. "As an entrepreneur trying to really figure it out, it's about having that combination of creativity and optimism and having faith that eventually it's going to work out in the end."

In 1999, Hsieh set out to become the online market leader in shoes. In 2003, he pivoted his vision to focusing on customer service and customer experience rather than a specific product. In 2005, he made corporate culture the number one priority of the company. Under his leadership, Zappos proactively and purposely set out to prioritize and redefine corporate culture. The entire company spent a year defining the culture and core values. Hsieh set the mission of Zappos as "delivering happiness," which later became the title of his book in 2013.

In 2013, Hsieh had his own AHA! moment of bringing customer and employee satisfaction together under the general happiness rubric. "We took a step back and realized customer service and that personal approach is about making customers happy and our culture is all about making employees happy. So really, let's try to tie it all together and have Zappos be about just delivering happiness in general, whether it's to customers or employees or to vendors," said Hsieh at the same business innovation summit.

This led to the launch of a broad platform called Zappos Insights. Zappos Insights created a series of thought leadership and online tools to allow other companies to adopt what Hsieh called "happiness as a business model." In 2014 he went on a multi-city tour and became the face of corporate happiness across America. He and his team of nine others hit the road on the "Happiness Bus" with the goal of inspiring others across the country. He was excited to be a thought leader and guru of happiness. Not only did he bring this message to the world, but thousands of business leaders and government officials visited Zappos' zany Las Vegas headquarters to tour the unique and fun offices and learn from Hsieh.

As Hsieh built a larger-than-life culture predicated on happiness, he also realized happiness required a more holistic, mental health approach. In 2016 he began working with folk singer Jewel, who had become focused on topics of mental health. Hsieh and Jewel created an online portal at Zappos called "Whole Human" with mental health tools and resources for employees.

While happiness was a core value Hsieh focused on and preached about at Zappos, it appeared he was struggling to define it for himself. In 2020, Hsieh moved from Las Vegas to a seventeen-thousand-square-foot mansion in Park City where he was trying to build a tech utopia. Things began to spiral quickly for him shortly thereafter. Jewel visited Hsieh in Park City in mid-August when she and other employees discovered the mansion in complete disarray. Candles were dripping all over the furniture, carpet, and other parts of the house. Dog droppings were scattered around. Jewel discovered Hsieh in the backyard in his boxer shorts thinner than she had ever seen him. He appeared to be abusing drugs including nitrous oxide.

In November 2020 he died at the age of forty-six in a house fire in Connecticut. The precise circumstances surrounding the fire and his death remain unclear. "It is possible that carelessness or even an intentional act by Hsieh could have started this fire," the fire report said. The fire was ruled an accident. Whether or not it was intentional will never be known. However, what is clear is that the self-proclaimed and widely respected guru on corporate happiness struggled with his own happiness right up to his untimely death (Business Innovation Factory 2014; Grind and Sayre 2022).

Many people go through life doing things they really don't want to and pushing off happiness to the future. It isn't a priority. For some, it takes a major life AHA! moment to make happiness in the present a top priority. This is unfortunate as you don't need a major setback or AHA! moment to make a deliberate choice to live a happier life.

Rather than living a life of perceived happiness or choosing to delay gratification to the future, my friend Chris transformed his view and approach to life and focuses on living every minute in the present.

YOU START DYING THE MOMENT YOU ARE BORN

"So, the doctor came in and asked, 'Who is the husband?' because there were probably twenty-five or thirty people in this hospital waiting room. And my father said, 'Me.' The doctor handed my father the wedding ring and the engagement ring and said, 'I'm sorry.' And everyone just lost it," explained Chris.

Chris was on the "overachiever" track his entire life leading up to this pivotal moment. A straight-A student in high school who then graduated at the top of his class in college, Chris had his sights set on climbing the corporate ladder. In college, he received a prestigious offer to join one of the big five accounting firms, Coopers & Lybrand. He was honored and excited and he accepted it. But exactly thirty days after graduating from college, his life and perspective changed forever.

He was out the night before in Philadelphia celebrating and enjoying life as a recent college graduate. At about 8 a.m. on July 2, 1988, Chris's dad woke him. Chris was still foggy from the night before when his father said, "It's your mother; come downstairs." His mom had fallen and was in distress with foam coming out of her mouth. He held his mom as he waited for the paramedics to arrive.

"She was forty-five years old. Died of a sudden heart attack. She died in my arms. And at that moment, it was the best moment of my life and the worst. I miss my mother, but she gave me the gift of living."

"After that day, I no longer focused on climbing the ladder but on living every day as if it is my last. And commuting for three hours and putting in a ten-hour workday no longer seemed attractive. So, I have a vivid memory of my mother's funeral saying to myself in a very private moment, as I went up to her casket thinking... *You lived, you lived, you lived*. And she did! 'So, I am sorry to see you go, but you've taught me that lesson to live.' That was my AHA! moment. If my mom was still here, I'd probably be sitting at a desk on Wall Street, miserable. At fifty-six years of age now, there is not a day I don't think of my mother and realize I am enjoying a day she never saw."

Today, Chris is quick to tell you he lives a happy life. He refuses to work a traditional corporate job and won't waste time doing things that won't make him happy. He is an entrepreneur and has found success in various businesses. He is also quick to say "yes" when friends and family invite him to events and activities.

Chris is convinced his mom's death made him a better parent. He is close to his kids. He brags about taking them to school and being at every event. Not only that, but he notes how many other fathers aren't there for their kids and finds this disappointing.

He recounts a golf trip he was on with buddies that happened to overlap with his daughter's dance recital. Both were important to him, and he wasn't going to miss either. He drove over four hours roundtrip to see his daughter perform for about four minutes. "Her eyes. She wept because I made it. She wept because she knew how far away I was. It's a memory that is ingrained in my brain forever."

"If I'm not happy, I'm going to waste away. I created a philosophy for myself. The moment you start dying is the moment you're born. So *live*. And my mom's death kind of was like her way of shaking my shoulders and saying, 'Look what happened to me.' So, every day I live. Every day I live after the day she died is a gift," Chris said.

For Chris, it took the death of his mother to change his approach and perspective on life. For BJ Miller, it took a near-death experience.

A JOLT TO LIFE
"We all need a reason to wake up."

During his sophomore year of college, just back from Thanksgiving break, BJ Miller was hanging out with friends and exploring when he climbed on top of a parked commuter train. He reached up and touched an overhead wire and was jolted with eleven thousand volts of electricity. As a result of the electric shock, BJ lost both his legs and an arm. It changed his life forever. "That night began my formal relationship with death," said BJ in a

2015 TED Talk. For BJ, this AHA! moment changed his perspective more than anything else.

"So much of what we're talking about today is a shift in perspective. After my accident, when I went back to college, I changed my major to art history. Studying visual art, I figured I'd learn something about how to see—a really potent lesson for a kid who couldn't change so much of what he was seeing. Perspective, that kind of alchemy we humans get to play with, turning anguish into a flower."

Today, he is a hospice and palliative care physician at Zen Hospice Project in San Francisco. Having been so close to death, BJ views it differently. BJ talks about a little ritual they have at Zen. "When one of our residents dies, the mortuary men come, and as we're wheeling the body out through the garden, heading for the gate, we pause. Anyone who wants—fellow residents, family, nurses, volunteers, the hearse drivers too, now—shares a story or a song or silence, as we sprinkle the body with flower petals. It takes a few minutes; it's a sweet, simple parting image to usher in grief with warmto rather than repugnance."

BJ contrasts this approach to the more traditional perspective of death in a hospital setting filled with beeping machines, blinking, and bright lights. This image is more institutional as the body is whisked away and the room is cleaned and turned for the next "resident." It is characterized by sterility and numbness.

It is not just at death that BJ has changed his perspective. "Beauty can be found anywhere. I spent a few months in a burn unit at St. Barnabas Hospital in Livingston, New Jersey, where I got really great care at every turn, including good palliative care for my pain. And one night, it began to snow outside. I remember my nurses complaining about driving through it. And there was no window in my room, but it was great to just imagine it coming down all sticky. Next day, one of my nurses smuggled in a snowball for me. She brought it in to the unit. I cannot tell you the rapture I felt holding that in my hand, and the coldness dripping onto my burning skin—the miracle of it all, the fascination as I watched it melt and turn into water. In that moment, just being any part of this planet in this universe mattered more to me than whether I lived or died. That little snowball packed all the inspiration I needed to both try to live and be okay if I did not."

Little things matter a lot, as BJ goes on to explain how he learns from residents at Zen. And it turns out, little things aren't always that little. He gives an example of one resident who has ALS and wants to smoke again. She wants to feel her lungs filled while she has them. Another resident just wants to have her dog at the foot of her bed. She wants to feel her dog against her dry skin. And he talks about how the most poignant room at the hospice is the kitchen. Baking cookies evokes all the senses. He refers to all these examples as small, instant rewards for just being.

BJ is grateful for the AHA! moment he had and how it changed his perspective. "I got to redesign my life around this fact, and I tell you it has been a liberation to realize you can always find a shock of beauty or meaning in what life you have left, like that snowball lasting for a perfect moment, all the while melting away. If we love such moments ferociously, maybe we can learn to live well—not in spite of death but because of it. Let death be what takes us, not lack of imagination."

Live today; don't wait for tomorrow. LITSG encourages each of us to live in the moment and make the most of every minute. Looking ahead to the end of your life and reflecting on how you want to be remembered will give you the framework for how to live your life to the fullest today. So, how do you want to be remembered?

LITSG REFLECTIONS

1. How often do you spend an inordinate amount of time reflecting on the past or worrying about the future? Live today. Make a conscious and deliberate effort to make today the best day ever. What do you have to do today to *live* today?

2. We often look to others with envy and benchmark ourselves relative to their perceived happiness. In doing so, we forget others are dealing with their own issues and might very well be creating an image of happiness within a life of sadness. How often to you spend more time focusing on what others have or what others think of you, rather than living the life you want to live?

3. By looking to the end of life and thinking about how you want to be remembered, you have a tool for

defining what is important to you today. Take some time to craft the message you want on your tombstone and to write both your eulogy and obituary. What are the key themes and messages? Are you living a life today that is consistent with these key themes and messages?

4. What is one thing you keep thinking about as an opportunity for happiness and life satisfaction in the future? What can you do right now to make this future hope, goal, or dream a reality today?

CHAPTER 12:

LIVING THE LITSG LIFE

That's been one of my mantras—focus and simplicity. Simple can be harder than complex: You have to work hard to get your thinking clean to make it simple. But it's worth it in the end because once you get there, you can move mountains.

—STEVE JOBS

AHA! LITSG, a simple but powerful philosophy and way of living. A collective AHA! moment right now as we come to the end of our LITSG journey together. Today is your opportunity to begin your LITSG journey. It is not hard, but it is life changing and empowering. You have the ability to live a happier and more fulfilling life and make the world a better place. Today is your day to start.

THE REARVIEW MIRROR: MY LITSG JOURNEY

Now that we traveled on the LITSG journey together, let's revisit how the path of my life helped me create this philosophy.

My LITSG journey had four major AHA! moments. The first was my father's heart attack in 1984 when I was ten years old. While I couldn't completely comprehend the magnitude of the situation, seeing my dad in a hospital bed and watching him recover forced me to reflect on how precious life is and how short it can be. Hearing his voice for the first time after he had triple bypass surgery was one of the most poignant and defining moments of my life. At the young age of ten, I already realized no one is guaranteed a tomorrow and today is the best day I have, so make the most of it.

While I had many more influential moments along the way, the next major AHA! moment came on September 11, 2001. On that beautiful fall morning, I walked by the World Trade Center in lower Manhattan less than an hour before terrorists would crash two commercial airliners into the buildings. Just a few blocks north, I looked on with shock and fear as the second plane flew low over the Hudson River and careened into the building. I fled the city that day and waited anxiously as friends and family checked in. What I experienced that day, and in the weeks after, changed my perspective on life and priorities. These events reinforced what I had learned, and sadly forgotten, when my father had his heart attack. Life is short, and tomorrow is not guaranteed. Do what you love and spend your very precious minutes wisely. Jenn and I sped up our timeline for starting a family and for the first time I prioritized life and family over a career and success in the workplace.

On March 30, 2007, my brother called me and said, "He is gone." Three words that changed my life and perspective forever as my father's death was the next major AHA! moment of my life. I grew up a lot that day and in the months that followed as I learned to live without him. Losing a close loved one really motivated and inspired me to live my best life. I truly understood how few minutes I had in my life and how I wanted to make the most of each precious one. I really appreciated the community support and the power of social networks. I appreciated all that I had and refused to dwell on what was lost. I focused on the good that life has to offer and worked hard to make sure I was enjoying a happy and fulfilling life. Burying my father and cleaning out the home I grew up in drove home my LITSG philosophy. I am both saddened by and grateful for these events and the lessons I learned.

Finally, on October 21, 2017, I was walking to a tailgate at the Rutgers president's house before a homecoming game when my brother called to tell me our mom had just passed away. This time it was a bit different than the call I received a decade earlier when I learned about my father's passing. The shock was less, but the pain was as great, if not greater. Realizing both my parents were now gone, refocused me on prioritizing time with friends and family. I had a finite time to be the best parent, spouse, and friend I could be. I became maniacally focused on enjoying quality time with people I love. Life is too short, and my mom's death reinforced my commitment to making the most of every minute.

ROADMAP TO YOUR LITSG JOURNEY

I am on a mission. I am going to make the world happier, one smile at a time. LITSG is a holistic philosophy, a way of living each day. It is simple and powerful. Every person can benefit from this way of life. You have the ability to make every day the best day ever with these simple and practical tools.

- *The power of positivity: Attitude is everything.* Positive thoughts lead to positive words, which lead to positive behaviors. Every day you wake up is a new beginning and a new opportunity. Make your first thought a positive one, and tell the world what a great day it is. Spread happy thoughts to others. Regardless of the facts and circumstances, use a lens of positivity and find the good in everyone and everything. Gratefulness is vital to happiness. View the world with extreme gratefulness, not superficial or forced gratefulness. Realize how lucky you are for what you have and acknowledge that no matter what, it can always be worse. Live every day as the best day of your life.

- *Choose your attitude; own it.* Now that you see the world through a lens of positivity, set a positive tone with others. Every interaction is an opportunity to set the tone. Think about how you approach emails, negotiations, and disagreements. Even the most aggressive, nastiest, unhappiest people are humans too and will more often react better to a positive tone and approach than a negative one. Use positive words in written and verbal communication. Also, remember that everyone has a personal story. Get to know strangers, service providers, and the world around you. It is a natural human desire to want to share our personal stories and interests. Engage people as humans and show empathy and a desire to hear their story. Be a leader every day, and have a positive impact on those around you. Choose your attitude, and bring that attitude to the world around you.

- *Little things make a big difference.* Take advantage of small opportunities and changes in your life to be happier and more fulfilled. Start each day with a smile and smile often. Smiling makes you happier and makes others around you happier. Use symbols and triggers as daily reminders of happiness and gratefulness. Poems, quotes, pictures, or whatever helps you refocus on what is important. As we get caught up in the chaos of daily life, sometimes we forget. Symbols remind us. Whistle, sing, enjoy music. Perform random acts of kindness every day as doing so makes you happier and makes others happier. Celebrate small wins, big wins, all wins. Celebrate the mundane and the extraordinary. Celebrate life.

- *Funny things are everywhere.* Humor is so incredibly powerful. Don't let a day go by without laughing and making others laugh. Humor disarms people and often levels the playing field. Humor breaks down social barriers and invites people into groups and social settings. Everyone wants to laugh, and showing humor is an easy way to relate to others. Humor reminds us to not take ourselves, our situations, or life too seriously.

- *Minutes matter.* On average, you were born with approximately forty-two million minutes to work with in life. Many of those minutes are behind you now. As you look at the minutes you have left, picture a barrel with the minutes in it. Take minutes out and use them wisely to make yourself and others happy. Don't let minutes just leak out. Be deliberate and proactive in how you choose to use them. Set goals to make sure you are using your minutes the way you want to. Learn how to prioritize. Invariably, life will throw pivot moments at you, so be prepared to reprioritize. Dream! Dream of what you can do, what you can be, and what you can accomplish. Reach high and far, and use minutes to accomplish your dreams.

- *Learn, learn, learn.* Make every day an opportunity to learn something new. We have so many ways and places to learn. Be proactive and deliberate, and make sure you are learning each day. Have a growth mindset about learning. You have complete control over your ability to learn and improve. Intelligence and other personality traits can be developed over time. Embrace failures as learning events.

- *Take a chance and get it done today.* Everyone has dreams, hopes, and wishes. Too often, we make excuses for why we can't do something rather than reasons for why we can. Stop with the excuses and focus on why you can. Reframe fear and risk. Reframe fear to Focus Entirely on Alternative Responses. Most fears are irrational and excessive when you think about them carefully. Even if the worst thing happens, how bad is this outcome? Learn to view fear on a relative basis. Reframe risk to Resist Instinct and Start with Knowledge. Don't automatically focus on the worst possible outcome. Realistically assess the risk and use knowledge rather than instinct. One of the biggest regrets people have on their death bed is failing to chase dreams. Don't regret what you didn't do. Do it today.

- *Can't make it alone.* It is the most basic human need to feel loved and to love others. We all want a place to belong. No one can make it alone. No one. Be proactive, and build strong social networks. Social interaction is one of the key drivers of happiness. Start by investing in and strengthening your most important relationships. Often this is with family, but many times it can be with friends. As you branch out, build broader social networks. Everyone can be a friend. Treat the strangers in your life today as possible friends tomorrow. Be a friendship leader, and bring groups together to enjoy life. It is easy to talk about parties, adventures, and trips with friends, but a true friendship leader makes it happen. One of the longest-running studies of what makes a good life concludes that relationships matter more than anything, and good relationships keep us happier and healthier as we age. Reach out today and check in with someone who impacted your life. Surprise them and show them how important they are to you.

- *Passion*: Be passionate about something. Be passionate about many things. You choose what you love to do and what you care about. Don't be an observer in life. Be committed, and go all in on the things you love. Leave your mark and make the organization or interest you are committing to better because of you. It is easy to associate with an interest group or join an organization. But true happiness and fulfillment in life comes from being passionate. Show your "rah rah" spirit for something. Brand yourself and your identity in part around your passion. Passion takes real commitment and being passionate about something you love creates meaningful happiness.

- *Live today; don't wait for tomorrow.* At some point, we will all die. We don't know exactly when, but it is inevitable. Live each day and each minute knowing tomorrow is not promised. Stop waiting, and start doing. Think about how you want to be remembered. What will be the words on your tombstone? Write them down. What are the key themes you want to be remembered for in your eulogy and your obituary? Write them down. Now embrace those words and themes, and live that life today. Make today the day you eat at that special restaurant or drink that special bottle of wine. Today is the day you tell those you love how much you love them. Today is the day you take the risk and do something you have long wanted to do. Today is your day. Today is the best day ever, if you make it that way.

Take a deep breath, close your eyes, and smile. As you reopen your eyes (still smiling I hope), reflect on what your key takeaways are from reading this book. LITSG is not a one-size-fits-all philosophy. It is a framework for making every day the best day ever. Adapt the tools and philosophies that work for you.

Start today by making small changes in your actions, behaviors, thoughts, and perspectives. Over time, embrace a new way of living. LITSG is my mission to make the world happier one smile at a time. Help me spread this belief and be a part of the LITSG culture. Tell others what you learned, and encourage them to learn about and to live the LITSG life. We can all live a happier life, and we can all work together to help others live a happier life. I can't imagine any greater contribution to society or any greater way to make the world a better place. You now have this power. Make today the best day ever... and then do it again tomorrow.

ACKNOWLEDGMENTS

Mr. Life Is Too Short Guy! That's what Kevin McHugh called me on our second Zoom call after I hired him as my executive coach. I completed a few assessments, and he started the call with "Dude, you are Mr. Life Is Too Short Guy! Everything has to be done now, and everything is happy and positive." I knew this is how I lived my life, but I couldn't define it in a few words before this call. Thank you to Kevin for showing me the way.

I told Jenn about Kevin's new name for me, and she nodded in agreement. She said it was perfect, and it should be the title of my book. I looked at her funny and said, "What would that book be about?" But in her own little brilliant way, she planted the seeds and let me figure it out. She quietly and subtly "watered" the seeds, and shortly thereafter, I began an outline for the book you just read. She gave me that push I needed to finally accomplish a dream I had for many years. Everything I have done in life is in partnership with Jenn, and this is just another example. We make an amazing team. Thank you, Jenn.

The core principles of LITSG developed over my lifetime, and no one had a greater influence over me and my life philosophy than my family. I start with my mom and dad who gave me every opportunity in life to find success and happiness. They are the foundation and pillars on which everything I have today are built. While I wish they were here to see me publish this book and accomplish this dream, I am so grateful to have spent many wonderful years learning from them. Thank you, Gloria and Joe, for raising me as you did and for helping me learn the importance of happiness, positivity, and gratefulness early on in life. You built the foundation of LITSG.

One of the greatest things to happen to me ever was finding the love of my life and soulmate when I was sixteen years old. Jenn is responsible for so much of who I am today, and for this I am grateful. With Jenn came my amazing in-laws Doris and Steve. They have been parents to me for my entire adult life. Many of the principles of LITSG were learned from growing up with them. They have always been so incredibly supportive, and I am grateful they saw me publish this book. Thank you, Doris and Steve, for being there to support me nearly my entire life.

The LITSG philosophy focuses on how finite life is and how important it is to make the most of every minute. Embrace happiness today. So much of my happiness comes from raising my daughters Amanda and Jessica. Many of the stories I tell in this book involve them in some way. I am grateful to them for helping me make every day the best day ever. I hope they take the LITSG principles I have taught them and carry on my legacy to future generations. They are the future of my mission to *make the world happier, one smile at a time.*

My LITSG author community has been so incredibly important to making this book a reality. Thank you all so very much. In particular, my beta readers who provided meaningful feedback and suggestions to improve this book and make it what you just read. Thanks to Jason Altberger, Jeff Bucklew, June Forrest, Joe Gasparro, Chuck Herman, Jeffrey Kagan, Sandra Kenoff, Scott Kornfeld, David Landau, Carolyn Mastrangelo, Larry Metz, Kelley Nicholson-Flynn, Yanet Noble, Cristina Pape, Beth Paul, Steven Pivnik, Laura Rastogi, Sam Rastogi, Michelle Rodriguez, David Seiden, Sheryl Seiden, Jay Soled, Nicole Vaccaro, Katherine Vyse, and Rachel Wallins. Each provided me with thoughtful feedback and suggestions, which were reflected in this book.

During the presale campaign, I had a lot to learn about marketing, positioning, and social media. Thanks to Chris Poreda for helping me design and build the website and think through positioning and social media. Thanks to Kaitlin Womack for sharing her creative expertise. Thanks also to Eric Drath for helping me create an amazing marketing video and for being incredibly supportive of me throughout my writing journey.

I can't say enough good things about Eric Koester and the teams at Manuscripts LLC (Creator Institute, Book Creators) and New Degree Press. Thank you all for making this dream a reality. In particular, thanks to John Saunders, Sherman Morrison, Ilia Epifanov, Jacques Moolman,

Gjorgji Pejkovski, Brian Bies, Emily Kim, Amanda Brown, and Erinn Kemper for your guidance and support throughout my journey. This book would not be what it is without you. You made it great.

And finally, thank you so much to my entire author community. I am so grateful to all of you for your support and guidance and appreciate each of you.

Harris Aaron

Penny Ackerman

Lynn Adams

Anthony Albrecht

Jared Allen

Cindy and Jason Altberger

Andrew Altorfer

Jeff Appleby

Tara Artel

Tom Aschenbrenner

Timothy Aspinwall

Barry Bachenheimer

Sharon and Peter Balsamo

Luis Barreto

Amy Barrickman

Shari Bates

Anne Bearman

Genine Befumo-Masiuk

Anita and Mitchell Beinhaker

Chance Benbow

Frank and Pam Bennett

Stacy and Matt Bergerman

Michael Bewsey

Jane Bieneman

Adam Birnbaum

Terry and Douglas Blagdon

Kathryn Blake

Sasha Slocum and David Blechinger

Blueprint Healthcare Real Estate Advisors

Blair and Kevin Borella

Drazen Bratic

Daniel Breslauer

Cheryl and Stuart Brown

Amy and Jeff Bucklew

Jennie Byrne

Samantha and Tony Calandra

Donovan Campbell

Venesha and Alan Cashdollar

Stephen Cassidy

Kristy and Jason Castelluccio

Joseph Catalano

Amanda and Adlai Chester

Michael Chodroff

Brian Cohen

Jasen Coldiron

Michelle and Darren
Composto

Michael Conlan

John Coyle

John Crocker

Chris and Anthony D'Angelo

Terri and Edward Davenport

Dennis Dechow

Oliver Dennison

Matt Dillon

Eric Drath

Konstantin Driker

Scott Eber

Doris and Steve Entin

Tracy and Dan Entin

Sue and Chris Evans

Wilson Fan

Frederick Favorule

Tim Fields

June and Wayne Forrest

Tracey and Benjamin Forrest

Mike Gallagher

Joseph Gasparro

John George

Taylor Gillan

Kristi Golden

Hari Chenglath

Cory Chmelka

Marc Citron

Matthew and Melissa Cohen

Francis Collins

Leigh Ann Conaway

Juan Copeland

David Crall

Jenn and John Czarnecki

Catherine and Arun Datwani

Laurent de Rosiere

Sean DeDeyn

Jaci and Bradley Diamond

Thomas Donnelly

Iain Drayton

Cheryl and Mike Eagan

Michael Engemann

Shannon and Paul Entin

Candice and Travis Epp

Michael Faber

Justin Farris

Dave Feltenberger

Lauren and Dan Forman

Stephanie and Brant Forrest

Stacie and Barry Friedman

Cisco Garcia

Tracy and Kevin Gehrt

Lauren and Ethan Giddings

Christian Giordano

Jen and Stephen Goldstein

David Goldstein

Heather and Larry Grimsley

Rachel and Jeff Guberman

Sandee and Jeet Guram

Mike Hennessy

Chuck Herman

Scott Higgs

Adam Holz

Tony Hornbach

Shari Hubert

David Indursky

Michael Iwanicki

Michael Jacobs

Rakesh Jain

Donna Jennings

Matthew Johnson

Roxane Kallensee

Lamees Kelley

Danny Kianmahd

Rich Knupp

Eric Koester

Ashish Kothari

Kathy LaMastra

Danielle and Josh Leibner

Jennifer Lewis

Gina Liebhauser

Stefanie and Eric Littman

Sonia and Pedro Loureiro

Bill MacKenzie

Craig MacPhail

Brian Graber

Kevin Groff

Steve Guberman

Scott Henkin

Michael Henriques

Matt Hershey

Lynn Holdsworth

Ken Hong

Stu Hothem

Andrea Hughes

Ron Iovino

Joshua Jacobs

Carrie and Jonathan Jaffe

Jillian and Greg Janaczek

Amanda Johnson

Jeffrey Kagan

Aaron Kaufman

Sandra and Eric Kenoff

Chris King

Janet Koenig

Pam and Scott Kornfeld

Kush Kothary

David Landau

Alex Leung

Jonathan Li

Daniel Lipper

Stacey and Josh Losardo

Rene Lubianski

Jerry Macnamara

Stephanie Mann

David Martin

Georgina Matthews

Patrick Mayer

Helen McEwen

Peter McGraw

Amisha Mehta

Mindi and Larry Metz

Elyse Michelson

Karen Miller

Emily Molitor

Roseita Monteiro

Jennifer Morgan

Jessica Morrow

Brendan Murray

Greg Myhre

Paula and Frank Natale

Brian Neuwirth

Kelley Nicholson-Flynn

Jon Northup

Brian O'Grady

Van Papadopoulos

John Papazoglou

Drew Pascarella

Mukesh Patel

Neal Patel

Beth and Kevin Paul

Merope Pentogenis

Brian Perkins

Joanne and Antonio Perrotta

Julie and Eric Peterson

Carolyn and Paul
Mastrangelo

Ashley Mattox

Timothy McCabe

Tracy and Joe McGinty

Caitlin McLaughlin

Eva Metcalf

Julie Michael

Ken Miller

David Miniman

Eric Moncik

Chris Moore

Alayne Morgenthal

Alyson and Henry Mroczko

Darren Mutnick

Uday Nandan

Russ Nesevich

Jason Newcomb

Yanet and Greg Noble

Keith Norton

Steve Ostergren

Mary Papamarkou

Cristina and Joseph Pape

Adrian and Mike Pastore

Hemanshu Patel

Dipak Patel

Doug Pedersen

Michael Peretz

Alyssa and Sean Perlman

John Petelik

Glenn Petriello

Jennifer and Pat Petrillo

Lindsey Phipps

Steven Pivnik

Ryan Pollock

Darren Powderly

Oscar Puig

Marla and Rick Radice

Raghunath Ram Mohan

Carl Rasmussen

Bob Raymond

George Rears

Karen and Tom Rendulich

Matt Rezkalla

Michelle Rodriguez

Edward Rosen

Rick Roth

Tony Rothermel

Steven Royzenshteyn

Michael Saffran

Ido Salama

Jerry Sanchez

Loren Altshuler and Andrew Sapira

Dori Saypol

Michael Seasonwein

Sheryl and David Seiden

Mark Sessing

Elizabeth Shaid

John Shewchuk

Kara and Ron Shovlin

Chitra Singh

Francine Pfeiffer

Michael Piloto

Bryan Pollack

Matthew Pomeroy

Leone Price

Michael Quadrino

Marc Radin

Amy and Joel Rampoldt

Laura and Sameer Rastogi

Edward Raymond

Cathy and Al Reicheg

Charles Renie

Charles Rigoglioso

James Rosebush

Rhoda Rosenberg

Michael Rothenberg

Maryellen Roy

Matt Rund

Powell Saks

Cyndi and Stephen Salemy

Joe Santagata

Valdi and Lauren Sapira

Sarah Scott

Erin Seguin Romano

Thomas Sessa

Dhiraj Shah

Elaine Sham

Mark Shore

Susan and Marty Shulman

Chrissy and Matt Skurbe

Mike Smith

Kate Snedeker

Amy and Jay Soled

Joe Speeney

Mark Spiro

David Stordy

Lisa and Mike Strug

Jonathan Swire

Daniel Tabor

Wray Thorn

Jeffrey Towers

Thaddeus Tracy

Nicole and Luke Vaccaro

Sunny Vanderbeck

Tuany Vo

Katherine Vyse

Riva and Sean Waller

Aaron Weigel

Debra and Craig Weinstein

Lisa Weisser

Lori and Jeff Wendler

Kevin White

Diana Wilmot

George Wolfe

Andrew Wright

Anthony Yoseloff

Mike Zimmer

Sharon Zydney

Katie Smith

Robin and Jeremy Soifer

Lisa and Abbey Spector

Chelsea Spickelmier

Mark Srulowitz

Daniel Stricker

Lauren and Robert Sutton

Ariel Szin

David Taglialatela

Rosemarie Thurston

Patrick Tracy

Elissa Levi and Michael Unger

Stefanie and Babak Vakili

Michael Viscusi

Glenn Votek

Andrew Wallace

Douglas Walters

Laura and Daniel Weinstein

Jennifer Weinstein

Jessica Weitzman

Rich Wenzel

Shane White

Jenn and Robb Wilner

Kaitlin Womack

Jamie Yackow

Allison Zaccherio

Amy Zuschke

APPENDIX:

REFERENCES

INTRODUCTION

American Psychological Association. 2022. "Stress in America: Money, Inflation, War Pile on to Nation Stuck in COVID-19 Survival Mode." https://www.apa.org/news/press/releases/ stress/2022/march-2022-survival-mode.

Cooban, Anna. 2021. "95% of Workers Are Thinking About Quitting Their Jobs, According to a New Survey—And Burnout Is the Number One Reason." *Insider.* July 7, 2021. https://www. businessinsider.com/labor-shortage-workers-quitting-quit-job-pandemic-covid-survey-monster-2021-7.

Ellis, Lindsay. 2022. "Harvard Wants M.B.A.s to Learn How to Be Happy at Work." *The Wall Street Journal*, February 14, 2022. https://www.wsj.com/articles/harvard-wants-m-b-a-s-to-learn-how-to-be-happy-at-work-11644836400.

Ettman, Catherine K., Gregory H. Cohen, Salma M. Abdalla, Laura Sampson, Ludovic Trinquart, Brian C. Castrucci, Rachel H. Bork, Melissa A. Clar, Ira Wilson, Patrick M. Vivier, and Sandro Galea. 2021. "Persistent depressive symptons during COVID-19: a national population-representative, longitudinal study of U.S. adults." *THE LANCET Regional Health Americas.* October 4, 2021. https://www.thelancet.com/journals/lanam/article/PIIS2667-193X(21)00087-9/fulltext.

National Institute of Mental Health. 2022. "Mental Health Information > Statistics." https://www.nimh.nih.gov/health/statistics/suicide.

National Science Foundation. 2005. Quoted in Stephanie Bogan, "Silence Those Voices in Your Head." InvestmentNews. November 30, 2016. https://www.investmentnews.com/silence-those-voices-in-your-head-69986.

NORC at The University of Chicago. 2020. "COVID Response Tracking Study." https://www.norc.org/PDFs/COVID%20Response%20Tracking%20Study/Historic%20Shift%20in%20Americans%20Happiness%20Amid%20Pandemic.pdf.

Sacerdote, Bruce, Ranjan Sehgal, and Molly Cook. 2020. "Why Is All COVID-19 News Bad News?" *National Bureau of Economic Research.* November 2020. https://www.nber.org/system/files/working_papers/w28110/w28110.pdf.

The World Health Organization. 2022. "WHO Coronavirus (COVID-19) Dashboard." https://covid19.who.int/.

CHAPTER TWO

Achor, Shawn. 2010. *The Happiness Advantage: The Seven Principles of Positive Psychology That Fuel Success and Performance at Work.* New York: Crown Business.

Lyubomirsky, Sonja, Kennon M. Sheldon, and David Schkade. 2005. "Pursuing Happiness: The Architecture of Sustainable Change." *Review of General Psychology.* June 1, 2005. https:// escholarship.org/uc/item/4v03h9gv.

Tracking Happiness. 2021. "Controlling Happiness Correlates With 32% Higher Happiness (New Study Results)." Updated March 17, 2021. https://www.trackinghappiness.com/controlling-happiness-new-study-results/.

CHAPTER FOUR

Coles, N. A., Jeff T. Larsen, and Heather C. Lench. 2019. "A Meta-Analysis of the Facial Feedback Literature: Effects of Facial Feedback on Emotional Experience Are Small and Variable." *Psychological Bulletin. 2019.* https://doi. org/10.1037/bul0000194.

Layton, Julia. 2009. "Does Singing Make You Happy?" *howstuffworks. June 2, 2009. https://science.howstuffworks.com/life/ inside-the-mind/emotions/singing-happy1.htm.*

McLean, Tamara. 2008. "Choral Singing Makes You Happy: Survey." *The Sydney Morning Herald.* July 20, 2008. https:// www.smh.com.au/national/choral-singing-makes-you-happy-survey-20080710-3cyg.html.

"Whistling While You Work a Lost Artistic Form." *The Daily Illini, February 7, 2012. https://dailyillini.com/life_and_culture-stories/2012/02/07/whistling-while-you-work-a-lost-artistic-form-2/.*

CHAPTER FIVE

Bitterly, T. Bradford, Alison Wood Brooks, and Maurice E. Schweitzer. 2017. "Risky Business: When Humor Increases and Decreases Status." *Journal of Personality and Social Psychology. 2017.* https://doi.org/10.1037/pspi0000079

Dowthwaite, Lowri. 2017. "A Sense of Humor Could Mean You're a Healthier, Happier, and Smarter Person." *Insider.* October 17, 2017. https://www.businessinsider.com/a-sense-of-humor-could-mean-youre-healthier-happier-and-smarter-2017-10.

CHAPTER SIX

Wendell, Bryan. 2015. "What Percentage of Boy Scouts Become Eagle Scouts?" *On Scouting.* March 30, 2015. https://blog.scoutingmagazine.org/2015/03/30/what-percentage-of-boy-scouts-become-eagle-scouts/.

CHAPTER SEVEN

Dweck, Carol S. 2006. *Mindset: The New Psychology of Success.* New York: Ballantine Books, an imprint division of Penguin Random House LLC, 2006, 2016.

CHAPTER EIGHT

Ware, Bronnie. 2011. *The Top five Regrets of the Dying: A Life Transformed by the Dearly Departing.* New York: Hay House, Inc.

CHAPTER NINE

DiJulio, Bianca, Liz Hamel, Cailey Munana, and Mollyann Brodie. 2018. "Loneliness and Social Isolation in the United States, the United Kingdom, and Japan: An International Study. The Kaiser Family Foundation. August 20, 2018.

https://www.kff.org/other/report/loneliness-and-social-isolation-in-the-united-states-the-united-kingdom-and-japan-an-international-survey/

Leland, John. 2022. "How Loneliness Is Damaging Our Health." *The New York Times.* April 20, 2022. https://www.nytimes.com/2022/04/20/nyregion/loneliness-epidemic.html

Mineo, Liz. 2017. "Good Genes Are Nice, but Joy Is Better." *The Harvard Gazette.* April 11, 2017. https://news.harvard.edu/gazette/story/2017/04/over-nearly-80-years-harvard-study-has-been-showing-how-to-live-a-healthy-and-happy-life/.

Parker-Pope, Tara. 2018. "The Power of Positive People." *The New York Times.* July 10, 2018. https://www.nytimes.com/2018/07/10/well/the-power-of-positive-people.html.

CHAPTER ELEVEN

Business Innovation Factory. 2014. "Tony Hsieh—Work Life Happiness? Zappos.com CEO Says You Bet." March 19, 2014. https://www.youtube.com/watch?v=EG2I5T1H6F4.

Grind, Kirsten and Katherine Sayre. 2022. "The Rise and Fall of the Management Visionary Behind Zappos." *The Wall Street Journal*. March 12, 2022. https://www.wsj.com/articles/the-rise-and-fall-of-the-management-visionary-behind-zappos-11647061122.

Miller, BJ. 2015. "What Really Matters at the End of Life." TED2015. https://www.ted.com/talks/bj_miller_what_really_matters_at_the_end_of_life/transcript?language=en.